WORLDVIEWS
IN
CONFLICT

Other Books by Ronald Nash

Beyond Liberation Theology
*Great Divides: 10 Controversies That Come
    Between Christians*
Poverty and Wealth
The Word of God and the Mind of Man
The Gospel and the Greeks
The Closing of the American Heart
Choosing a College
Faith and Reason: Searching for a Rational Faith
Social Justice and the Christian Church
Process Theology (editor)
Liberation Theology (editor)
Evangelical Renewal in the Mainline Churches
Christian Faith and Historical Understanding
The Concept of God
Evangelicals in America
Freedom, Justice and the State
*The Light of the Mind: St. Augustine's Theory
    of Knowledge*
Ideas of History (editor)
The Case for Biblical Christianity (editor)
The Philosophy of Gordon H. Clark (editor)
The New Evangelicalism
Dooyeweerd and the Amsterdam Philosophy

WORLD-VIEWS IN CONFLICT

CHOOSING CHRISTIANITY IN A WORLD OF IDEAS

RONALD H. NASH

ZondervanPublishingHouse

Academic and Professional Books

Grand Rapids, Michigan

A Division of HarperCollinsPublishers

WORLDVIEWS IN CONFLICT
Copyright © 1992 by Ronald H. Nash

Requests for information should be addressed to:
Zondervan Publishing House
Academic and Professional Books
Grand Rapids, Michigan 49530

Library of Congress Cataloging-in-Publication Data

Nash, Ronald H.
    Worldviews in conflict : choosing Christianity in the world of
ideas / Ronald H. Nash.
        p.   cm.
    Includes bibliographical references and index.
    ISBN 0-310-57771-3
    1. Apologetics—20th century. 2. Naturalism. 3. New Age
movement. I. Title.   92-9886
    BT1102.N37   1992   CIP

Edited by Robert D. Wood
Cover designed by Kurt Dietsch

Printed in the United States of America

95 96 97 98 99 / DH / 8 7 6 5 4

To
Gerald and Dolly
and
Their Family

Contents

PREFACE 8

1. WHAT IS A WORLDVIEW? 16

2. THE CHRISTIAN WORLDVIEW 34

3. HOW TO CHOOSE A WORLDVIEW 54

4. A FURTHER LOOK AT THE TEST OF REASON 73

5. CHRISTIANITY AND THE TEST OF REASON 93

6. A FURTHER LOOK AT THE PROBLEM OF EVIL 107

7. NATURALISM 116

8. THE NEW AGE MOVEMENT 130

9. THE INCARNATION AND THE RESURRECTION 147

10. WINNING THE BATTLE IN THE WORLD OF IDEAS 164

SUGGESTIONS FOR FURTHER READING 170

INDEX 174

Preface

As I passed the security guard and left the entrance of my Moscow hotel, I saw the bus that would shortly take me and the group of which I was a part to my first lecture in the Soviet Union. It was May 1991—just a few weeks before the abortive coup that unintentionally hastened the end of Soviet Communism. I was in Moscow as part of a team that had been invited by the Russian Ministry of Education to speak to hundreds of school teachers. None of us quite knew what to expect from the officials who escorted us nor, for that matter, from our audience.

It was a tremendous opportunity. In fact, as I approached the bus and our escorts, I could not help but think that everything else I had done up to this point in my life was preparation for this day. The decades of study and teaching, the degrees, the writing and publishing—all of it was like training in the minor leagues. I felt like the rookie who comes to bat for the first time in the majors.

My task was to help ground my audience of university graduates in information that would help them explain the Christian faith to their students. That we were doing this at the invitation of and with the assistance of Russian governmental officials still astounds me. Since my participation was limited to two presentations, I was forced to ask myself how I could do the most good in such a short time frame. Other speakers would be discussing important facets of Christian belief. I decided that I could not do anything more important than to explain what we mean by the Christian worldview, and to contrast that with alien beliefs that have been so central to education in the Soviet Union since the communist takeover in 1917.

Those few days in Moscow were unforgettable. My efforts to contrast the biblical worldview with the atheism, materialism, naturalism, and relativism with which generations of Soviets had been indoctrinated did more than help those in my audience see a new way of approaching and understanding the world. For many of them it was a worldview they now wanted for their own.

It is sadly ironic that the basic features of the naturalistic worldview, which so many people in the formerly Marxist nations are now rejecting, remain attractive to great numbers of educated people in the West. One major reason for this, I am convinced, is that few Americans have been taught to think in terms of worldviews. They do not know what a worldview is; they could not spell out the content of their own worldview if their lives depended on it; they are unaware of how various aspects of conflicting worldviews clash logically.

Basically, what I attempt in this book is to communicate the same message I gave my audiences in the Soviet Union. Raising one's level of self-consciousness about worldviews is an essential part of intellectual maturity. But I also want the reader to acquire a clearer understanding of the content of the Christian worldview. Following that, I offer brief accounts of the two worldviews that in the United States are the major challengers to the Christian perspective. One of those competitors is called naturalism. As we will see, naturalism resonates with important elements of the old Marxist worldview. In fact, Marxism has been one of the dominant expressions of naturalism in the twentieth century.

The other competing worldview I examine is the so-called New Age Movement, which continues to gain large numbers of followers. In most respects, New Age thinking contradicts naturalism, and is antithetic to almost everything that informed, biblically sound Christians believe. It is also worth noting that as the people of the Soviet Union turn away from Marxism, New Age beliefs are filling up the resulting worldview vacuum.

I had originally thought of titling this book *Winning the Battle in the World of Ideas*. There was no intent on my part to suggest any note of triumphalism in these words. By no means was I suggesting that the battle had been won or that victory was just around the next corner. Active, thinking Christians are involved in battles every day of their lives. While it is understandable that most Christians tend to think of this battle in its moral and spiritual dimensions, here I deal with the intellectual side of the conflict. This is a fight we do not want to *lose*; hence, my concern to provide a blueprint for how we might do a better job to prepare ourselves to perform effectively in the world of ideas.

The idea for this book originated with the manager of a bookstore in Boise, Idaho. This man and some of his friends in a study group had found a number of my earlier writings helpful as they wrestled with several important issues. He suggested that I consider adapting some of these writings to a more popular audience. This book is a response to his good idea.

I have written, therefore, with the needs and interests of the general reader in mind. But I have also designed the book to be useful as a supplementary textbook in college and seminary courses where an introduction to worldview thinking is presented. While I have tried my best to make the arguments of the book accessible to as many readers as possible, I have had difficulty reaching this goal in a few spots where issues are unusually complex. Simplifying is one thing; oversimplifying is another. The toughest part here is chapter five. There I deal with two knotty challenges to the Christian faith, namely, the claims that the faith is logically contradictory because of its insistence that Jesus Christ is fully God and fully man plus the additional assertion that the existence of evil in the world is logically incompatible with the nature of the Christian God. There is no way to deal with these challenges that is, at the same time, both simple and responsible. My advice to the reader, therefore, is not to get bogged down in this chapter. Then, after completing the book, return to chapter five and work through the material or simply remember where those arguments are if they are ever needed. One can live a rich, full, and happy life without understanding every single point in chapter five.

Most of the Christians I know love challenges of one kind or another. They may take up jogging and strive to run a certain distance in a specific time, or they may try to shoot a round of golf under eighty, or climb a mountain. Or, to mention one of life's greatest feats, they may decide to raise a family.

To me, it is a great mystery why so many people who respond heroically to other challenges shun those so abundant in the world of ideas. While many of us push our bodies to the limit, any unnecessary use of our minds is treated with the same disdain we gave, when children, to eating spinach or broccoli. I would like to think that this book will somehow end up in the hands of thousands of men and women who will begin to exercise their minds, who will become mentally alert and prepared, who will become more conscious of the battle in the world of ideas, and who will be equipped to begin winning that battle.

Most Christians are familiar with these words from Paul:

> [B]e strong in the Lord and in his mighty power. Put on the full armor of God so that you can take your stand against the devil's schemes. For our struggle is not against flesh and blood, but against the rulers, against the authorities, against the powers of this dark world and against the spiritual forces of evil in the

heavenly realms. Therefore put on the full armor of
God, so that when the day of evil comes, you may be
able to stand your ground. . . . (Eph. 6:10–13)

Despite the familiarity of this passage, many of us fail to
understand the full range of Paul's thoughts. We know that
he goes on to enumerate various elements of the Christian's
armor, such as the breastplate of righteousness and the
shield of faith and the helmet of salvation. But we
frequently fail to relate all this armor to a basic question:
why would anyone need defensive armor like this along
with the one offensive weapon mentioned in the text, the
sword of the Spirit, which is the Word of God? The answer
is simply this: *Christians need armor because they are
combatants in a war.*

But even when that point is grasped, some Christians
err by failing to see the full dimensions of this battle. Some
are often so preoccupied with "higher" things or "spiritual"
things—being otherworldly minded—that even on those
occasions when they realize the Christian life involves
them in a kind of war, they tend to think of that warfare
only in spiritual and moral terms. Far be it from me to
denigrate *that* dimension of the Christian's warfare; it *is*
spiritual and moral. But it is something more. And it is this
other dimension of the Christian's involvement in warfare
that I want to focus on in this book.

From its inception, the Christian church has been
involved in battles involving ideas, theories, systems of
thought, presuppositions, and arguments. Signs of such
battles in the world of ideas can be found all through the
New Testament. They occur in the Gospels in the question
of Jesus' identity. "Who do people say the Son of Man is?"
Jesus asked Peter (Matt. 16:13). They occur early in the
book of Acts over the fact of Christ's bodily resurrection.
They arise in connection with Christianity's relationship to
Old Testament law: Must one become a good Jew in order
to be a good Christian? To be a Christian, must one obey
Old Testament law? And these signs of warfare in the world

of ideas also show up in cryptic New Testament references to beliefs that resemble elements of Gnosticism, a threat that developed more fully in the second century.[1]

The battle of ideas continued throughout the early centuries of the church as Christian leaders fought proponents of heretical ideas. These challenges to the faith forced the church to formulate and systematize its thinking about such important doctrines as the deity of Christ, the deity and personality of the Holy Spirit, and the Trinity. During the Reformation, the battle in the world of ideas concerned efforts to rescue the purity of New Testament belief from perversions of that teaching that had crept into the church during the Middle Ages. In the eighteenth century, the battle was joined over the unbelief rising from the Enlightenment. In the nineteenth century, the church dealt with challenges to the authority of the Bible and with new problems raised by Darwinism. Early in the twentieth century, Christians struggled against religious modernism.

During the first several decades of this century, conflicts in the world of ideas seemed removed from the everyday life of the average Christian. Those battles were usually fought in academic circles—the more prominent colleges and universities and in theological seminaries. Back then, when smaller numbers of Americans attended college, many average Christians tended to give little thought to these issues.

That inattention carried a high price tag, however. Eventually, the anti-Christian ideas that gained dominance in America's intellectual centers filtered down to many theological seminaries and finally took hold in the religion departments of many church-related colleges. It is sad that the process continues today, as many informed observers of self-described evangelical colleges and seminaries report. That unbelief also reached the pulpits of a number of formerly faithful churches. Because many people in the

[1]For more on this, see my *The Gospel and the Greeks: Was the New Testament Influenced by Pagan Thought?* (Dallas: Probe Books, 1992).

pews were theologically illiterate or indifferent, the fact that some pastors were now preaching a new gospel—one that denied practically every major tenet of New Testament faith—went unnoticed. America's mainline denominations were lost to liberalism and unbelief because in the century following the American Civil War the Christian church lost the battle in the world of ideas.

But this is *not* a book about those earlier battles, even though the Christian church must remain prepared to deal with old errors that continue to be propagated in some circles, including more than a few seminaries and college religion departments. Rather, this is a book about important steps Christians *today* must take to prepare themselves for intellectual battles that confront *us*.

The most important step for Christians is to become informed about the Christian worldview, a comprehensive, systematic view of life and of the world as a whole. No believer today can be really effective in the arena of ideas until he or she has been trained to think in worldview terms. How does the Christian worldview differ from worldviews of the enemy? What are the weaknesses of competing worldviews? How can we utilize the best arguments against them?

Chapter one introduces the reader to the notion of a worldview. What is a worldview? Why is it important to think in worldview terms? Chapter two builds upon the earlier discussion and develops a clear and careful analysis of the Christian worldview. Chapter three offers three widely recognized tests to help believers make rational choices among competing worldviews. It would be intellectual suicide to think that all worldviews are equally plausible and worthy of belief.

One of the three tests to which every worldview should be subjected is the test of reason, namely, the law of noncontradiction. Chapter four takes a further look at this test and, among other things, advises Christians not to regard reason or logic as an enemy of faith. Since it is vitally important that Christianity pass the test of reason, it is a

matter of some urgency that Christians be able to defend
their faith from allegations that it is in some way self-
contradictory. Two challenges from this direction are
evaluated in chapter five, namely, the claim that the
existence of evil in the world is logically incompatible with
the Christian's belief in an all-powerful, all-knowing, and
good God, along with the assertion that the Christian belief
that Jesus is both God and man violates the law of
noncontradiction. The reader is offered as simple an answer
as possible to both charges.

If the Christian faith is to hold its own in the arena of
ideas, it must be able to deal satisfactorily with other issues
raised by the problem of evil. Accordingly, chapter six takes
a further look at that difficult area and provides the
Christian reader additional help.

Chapter seven examines what has been Christianity's
chief competitor in the Western world to date, the worldview known as naturalism. Chapter eight explains and
evaluates its newest challenger, the New Age Movement.
These two chapters conclude that both naturalism and New
Age thought suffer from serious problems that ought to
disqualify them as viable options in the world of ideas.

Chapter nine examines the case that can be made to
support the basic Christian beliefs of the incarnation and
the resurrection of Christ. Mastery of this information can
enable Christians to move from a defensive posture and go
on the offensive. Chapter ten concludes our discussion by
noting two other steps that people interested in doing battle
in the world of ideas must take.

Every week I learn of people whose Christian thinking
has been revitalized by the information contained here.
Believers untrained in worldview thinking are like a boxer
with one arm tied behind him. Their desire to perform well
is hampered by unnecessary limitation; in this case, a lack
of access to basic tools. My purpose is to provide those
tools, the most important of which is the ability to think in
terms of worldviews.□

Chapter 1

What Is a Worldview?

In its simplest terms, a worldview is a set of beliefs about the most important issues in life. The philosophical systems of great thinkers such as Plato and Aristotle were worldviews. Every mature rational human being, each reader of this book, has his or her own worldview just as surely as Plato did. It seems sometimes that few have any idea what that worldview is or even that they have one. Yet achieving awareness of our worldview is one of the most important things we can do to enhance self-understanding, and insight into the worldviews of others is essential to an understanding of what makes them tick.

Implicit in all this is the additional point that these beliefs must cohere in some way and form a system. A fancy term that can be useful here is *conceptual scheme*, by which I mean a pattern or arrangement of concepts (ideas). A worldview, then, is a conceptual scheme by which we consciously or unconsciously place or fit everything we believe and by which we interpret and judge reality.

One of the more important things we can do for others is to help them achieve a better understanding of their worldview. We can also assist them to improve it, which means eliminating inconsistencies and providing new information that will help fill gaps in their conceptual system. University of Michigan philosopher George Mavrodes shares this view of the importance of worldview thinking:

> Providing a man with a conceptual framework in which he can see his whole life as being lived in the presence of God is analogous to teaching a man to read a strange script. We can give him a key, a sort of Rosetta stone, by telling him the meaning of one particular inscription. If he believes us he can then understand that inscription. But the test of whether he has really learned how to read the script, and also the confirmation that the translation we gave him was accurate, comes when he encounters all the other inscriptions that are scattered through his world. If he cannot read them, then he has not yet learned that language and he is still subject to the doubt that what we gave him may not have been a translation at all, but rather a message quite unrelated to what was written.[1]

Philosopher W. P. Alston offers another reason why worldviews are important:

> It can be argued on the basis of facts concerning the nature of man and the conditions of human life that human beings have a deep-seated need to form some general picture of the total universe in which they live, in order to be able to relate their own fragmentary activities to the universe as a whole in a way meaningful to them; and that a life in which this is not carried through is a life impoverished in a most significant respect.[2]

The right eyeglasses can put the world into clearer focus, and the correct worldview can function in much the

[1]George Mavrodes, *Belief in God* (New York: Random House, 1970), 86. The Rosetta stone is a stone tablet on which an Egyptian decree of 196 B.C. was inscribed in three languages: Greek, Egyptian hieroglyphic, and Demotic. Discovered near the Egyptian town of Rosetta in 1799, this important archaeological find provided the key for the deciphering of Egyptian hieroglyphics.

[2]W. P. Alston, "Problems of Philosophy of Religion," in *The Encyclopedia of Philosophy*, reprint (New York: Macmillan, 1972), 6:286.

same way. When someone looks at the world from the perspective of the wrong worldview, the world won't make much sense to him. Or what he thinks makes sense will, in fact, be wrong in important respects. Putting on the right conceptual scheme, that is, viewing the world through the correct worldview, can have important repercussions for the rest of the person's understanding of events and ideas.

Most of us know people who seem incapable of seeing certain points that are obvious to us (perhaps those people view us as equally obtuse or stubborn). They often seem to have a built-in grid that filters out information and arguments and that leads them to place a peculiar twist on what seems obvious to us. While sometimes this may be the result of something peculiar to them, it is usually a consequence of their worldview. The ability of some to be open to new beliefs is often a function of the conceptual system in terms of which they approach the world and the claims of others.

Many disagreements among individuals, societies, and nations are clashes of competing worldviews. This is certainly the case between advocates of the pro-life and pro-choice positions on abortion. It is also true with regard to the growing number of conflicts between secular humanists and religious believers.

It is probably rare when the worldviews of two people match in every important detail. It may be helpful to think of different worldviews as circles that overlap to a greater or lesser degree. The following three pairs of concentric circles illustrate the relationships among three sets of worldviews.

The two circles above represent two worldviews that are similar on most issues. As an example, they might represent the conceptual schemes of two theologically conservative Christians from different denominations. Even though two such people will understandably disagree about many things, nonetheless they share a common commitment to the central beliefs of the Christian worldview.

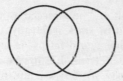

The next pair of circles pictures the worldviews of two people who disagree more than they agree.

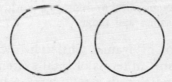

The two circles above do not overlap at all. They may represent the disparate worldviews of General Norman Schwartzkopf and Saddam Hussein. A bit of pastoral advice: two people whose worldviews are represented by our last pair of circles should not marry each other. A major and probably unresolvable clash of views is likely between two people whose worldviews fail to overlap at all.[3]

VIEWING CHRISTIANITY AS A WORLDVIEW

Instead of thinking of Christianity as a collection of theological bits and pieces to be believed or debated, we should approach our faith as a conceptual system, as a total world-and-life view. Once people understand that both Christianity and its adversaries in the world of ideas are

[3]While two or more individuals can hold worldviews that are generally alike, this situation would not require total agreement about everything they believe. One's worldview beliefs are restricted to a relatively small set of significant issues. Two people could share similar views of God, the universe, ethics, and so on. But they could disagree about many other issues (for example, whether they like alfalfa sprouts on their hamburgers).

worldviews, they will be in better position to judge the relative merits of the total Christian system. William Abraham has written:

> Religious belief should be assessed as a rounded whole rather than taken in stark isolation. Christianity, for example, like other world faiths, is a complex, large-scale system of belief which must be seen as a whole before it is assessed. To break it up into disconnected parts is to mutilate and distort its true character. We can, of course, distinguish certain elements in the Christian faith, but we must still stand back and see it as a complex interaction of these elements. We need to see it as a metaphysical system, as a worldview, that is total in its scope and range.[4]

The case for or against Christian theism[5] should be made and evaluated in terms of total systems. Christianity is not simply a religion that tells human beings how they may be forgiven, however important this information is. Christianity is also a total world-and-life view. Our faith has important things to say about the whole of human life. Once Christians understand in a systematic way how the options to Christianity are also worldviews, they will be in a better position to justify their choice of Christianity rationally. The reason many people reject our faith is not due to their problems with one or two isolated issues; it is the result of their anti-Christian conceptual scheme, which leads them to reject information and arguments that for believers provide support for the Christian worldview. Every worldview has questions it appears unable to answer satisfactorily. One might wish that all Christians were able effectively to defend their faith; therefore, our important task is to equip ourselves so that we are able to show

[4]William J. Abraham, *An Introduction to the Philosophy of Religion* (Englewood Cliffs, N.J.: Prentice-Hall, 1985), 104.
[5]The word *theism* applies to a belief in one supreme, all-knowing, all-powerful, personal God. Hence, one can distinguish among Christian, Jewish, and Muslim theism.

detractors that the Christian worldview is superior rationally, morally, and existentially[6] to any alternative system.

Because so many elements of a worldview are philosophical in nature, it is vital that Christians become more conscious of the importance of philosophy. Philosophy matters. It matters because the Christian worldview has an intrinsic connection to philosophy and the world of ideas It matters because philosophy is related in a critically important way to life, culture, and religion And it matters because the systems opposing Christianity use the methods and arguments of philosophy. Though philosophy and religion often use different language and often arrive at different conclusions, they deal with the same questions, which include questions about what exists (metaphysics), how humans should live (ethics), and how human beings know (epistemology).[7]

THE IMPORTANT ROLE OF PRESUPPOSITIONS

We all hold a number of beliefs that we presuppose or accept without support from other beliefs or arguments or evidence. Such presuppositions are necessary if we are to think at all. In the words of the Christian thinker Augustine (A.D. 354–430), we must believe something before we can know anything. Whenever we think, we simply take some things for granted. The consequences of a number of these presuppositions for philosophy and religion as well as for thinking in general are often significant.

Often beginning students of geometry tend to overlook

[6]My use of the word *existentially* here has nothing to do with any of the forms of existential philosophy. I am referring to the fact, explained shortly, that any worldview must be such that those who accept it intellectually can also live what they profess. Competing worldviews need to be tested both in the philosophy classroom and in the laboratory of life.

[7]I debated using technical terms like *metaphysics* and *epistemology* in this book. I finally decided that when a book talks about metaphysics (the study of ultimate reality) and epistemology (the philosophical examination of knowledge), informed readers will want to add the words to their vocabulary.

the significance of the axioms at the beginning of their textbook. They hurry over them in order to get into what they think is the more important work of solving problems. The axioms, while basic to all the subsequent proofs in the system, are themselves not proved or even provable. However, advanced students soon realize that with regard to the ultimate validity of all subsequent argumentation, these basic axioms are more important than the later problems and solutions. If the axioms are denied, the propositions deduced from the axioms do not follow since there is nothing for them to follow from; the validity of the entire system becomes suspect. In a similar way, human knowledge depends on certain assumptions that are often unexpressed, sometimes unrecognized, and frequently unproved.[8]

As Notre Dame philosopher Thomas Morris explains, the most important presuppositions in any person's system of beliefs

> are the most basic and most general beliefs about God, man, and the world that anyone can have. They are not usually consciously entertained but rather function as the perspective from which an individual sees and interprets both the events of his own life and the various circumstances of the world around him. These presuppositions in conjunction with one another delimit the boundaries within which all other less foundational beliefs are held.[9]

[8]While geometry provides a helpful illustration of the point I make about the importance of presuppositions, the analogy can be pressed too far and thus mislead. Geometric axioms function obviously in a deductive system. I am *not* suggesting that basic assumptions or presuppositions underlying a person's belief structure always or necessarily or even optimally function as axioms from which he then deduces the other elements of his worldview. In a variety of ways, presuppositions relate to other elements of a person's system of beliefs. Sometimes the relationship is deductive; often it is not.

[9]Thomas V. Morris, *Francis Schaeffer's Apologetics* (Grand Rapids: Baker, 1987), 109. I should make clear that Morris's remarks appear in the course of his exposition of Francis Schaeffer's views.

Even scientists make important epistemological, metaphysical, and ethical assumptions. They assume, for example, that knowledge is possible and that sense experience is reliable (epistemology), that the universe is regular (metaphysics), and that scientists should be honest (ethics). Without these assumptions, which scientists cannot verify within the limits of their methodology, scientific inquiry would soon collapse.

Basic assumptions or presuppositions are important because of the way they determine the method and goal of theoretical thought. They can be compared to a train running on tracks that have no switches. Once a person commits himself to a certain set of presuppositions, his direction and destination are determined. An acceptance of the presuppositions of the Christian worldview will lead a person to conclusions very different from those that would follow a commitment, say, to the presuppositions of naturalism.[10] One's axioms determine one's theorems.[11]

THE NONTHEORETICAL FOUNDATIONS OF THEORETICAL THOUGHT

While the title for this section may appear unnecessarily technical, it is the best language to introduce an intensely important point. A number of Christian writers have attempted to draw attention to the fact that the kinds of theoretical thinking we find in science, philosophy, and even theology are often strongly affected by nontheoretical considerations. It is hard to ignore the personal dimension that enters into one's acceptance and evaluation of a worldview, including a religious system like Christianity. It

[10]This claim assumes that the parties involved think and act consistently. We all know professing Christians whose judgments and conduct conflict with important principles of their faith. Many nontheists, often unconsciously, appear to draw back from positions that their presuppositions seem to entail.

[11]Once again a qualification may help avoid misunderstanding. In geometry this sentence is true literally. In a broader discussion of belief structures and worldviews, it is true generally.

23

would be foolish to pretend that human beings always handle such matters impersonally and objectively, without reference to considerations rooted in their psychological makeup. Many people demonstrate that they are often incapable of thinking clearly about their worldview. Most of us have met people or come across the writings of those who appear so captive to a conceptual scheme that they seem incapable of giving a fair hearing to any argument or bit of evidence that appears to threaten their system. This is true of both theists and nontheists.

Sometimes people have difficulty with competing claims and systems because of philosophical presuppositions. But often their theoretical judgments seem inordinately affected by nontheoretical factors. This is the case, for example, when racial prejudice causes people to hold certain untrue beliefs about those who are objects of the prejudice. Sometimes these nontheoretical factors are unique to the particular person, rooted in his or her personal history. Some writers have suggested that another type of nontheoretical influence affects our thinking. According to them, human thoughts and actions have religious roots in the sense that they are related to the human heart, the center of our attitude toward religion.[12] Human beings are never neutral with regard to God. Either we worship God as Creator and Lord, or we turn away from God. Because the heart is directed either toward God or against him, theoretical thinking is never so pure or autonomous as many would like to think. While this line of thinking raises questions that cannot be explored further in this book, it does seem that some who appear to reject

---

[12]I regret the need to resort to metaphors at this point. But we are on difficult terrain. Although the basic point seems true, it is very difficult to sort out all the issues. For an example of one writer who argued for this position, see Herman Dooyeweerd's *In the Twilight of Western Thought* (Philadelphia: Presbyterian and Reformed, 1960). For a nontechnical introduction to Dooyeweerd's work, see my *Dooyeweerd and the Amsterdam Philosophy* (Grand Rapids: Zondervan, 1962). For a later critique of Dooyeweerd, see my *The Word of God and the Mind of Man* (Phillipsburg, N. J.: Presbyterian and Reformed, 1992).

Christianity on rational or theoretical grounds are, in fact, acting under the influence of nonrational factors; that is, more ultimate commitments of their hearts. People should be encouraged to dig below the surface and uncover the basic philosophical and religious presuppositions that often appear to control their thinking.

Though the influence of nontheoretical factors on people's thinking is often extensive, it is never total in the sense that it precludes life-altering changes. The case of Saul of Tarsus—one of early Christianity's greatest enemies, a person fanatically committed to a system that seemed to rule out any possibility of his change or conversion—encourages us to believe that no one is incapable of change. People do change conceptual systems. Conversions take place all the time. People who used to be humanists or naturalists or atheists or followers of competing religious faiths have found reasons to turn away from their old conceptual systems and embrace Christianity. Conversely, people who used to profess allegiance to Christianity reach a point where they feel they can no longer believe.

Of course, we must also recognize that many changes regarding worldviews have little or nothing to do with Christian conversion. Even the noted Christian writer C. S. Lewis admits that he abandoned a naturalistic worldview in favor of an intellectual acceptance of the Christian worldview months before his actual conversion.[13] In spite of all the obstacles I have noted, people do occasionally begin to doubt conceptual systems they had accepted for years. And sometimes, as we know, people make dramatic changes in their belief systems.

Is it possible to identify a single set of necessary conditions that will always be present when people change a worldview? I doubt it. After all, as I have pointed out, many people remain unaware that they have a worldview,

---

[13]Of course, it would be natural for any Christian to see Lewis's intellectual conversion as a God-directed stage in what eventually became his spiritual conversion.

even though the sudden change in their lives and thoughts resulted from their exchanging one worldview for another. It does seem clear that dramatic changes like this usually require time for one to work through doubts about key elements of the worldview. Even when the change appears to have been sudden, it was in all likelihood preceded by a period of growing uncertainty and doubt. In many cases, the actual change is triggered by a significant event, often a crisis of some kind. But I have also heard people recount stories that laid out different scenarios. Suddenly, or so it seemed, an event or piece of new information led them to think in terms of a conceptual scheme that was totally different for them. Quite unexpectedly, these people "saw" things they had overlooked before, or they suddenly "saw" matters fit together in a pattern that brought meaning where none had been discernible before.

People are different; systems of belief are different. People change their minds on important subjects for a bewildering variety of reasons (or nonreasons). It is foolish, therefore, to try to cram all the possibilities and reasons for life-transforming changes into any given pattern.

THE MAJOR ELEMENTS OF A WORLDVIEW

What kinds of beliefs make up a worldview? A well-rounded worldview includes beliefs in at least five major areas: God, reality, knowledge, morality, and humankind.

God

The most important element of any worldview is what it says or does not say about God. Worldviews differ greatly on this matter. Does God even exist? What is the nature of God? Is there only one true God? Is God a personal being, that is, is God the kind of being who can know, love, and act? Or is God an impersonal force or power? Because of conflicting views about the nature of God, such systems as

Buddhism, Hinduism, Shintoism, and Zoroastrianism are not only different religions; they embrace different worldviews.[14] Because Christianity, Judaism, and Islam are examples of theism, conservative adherents of these religions hold to worldviews that have more in common than they do with dualistic, polytheistic, and pantheistic systems.[15] One essential component, then, of any worldview is its view of God.

It would be a mistake to regard self-described atheists as an exception to the points made in the previous paragraph. If we understand a person's God to be that which is one's ultimate concern, then there really is no such thing as an atheist. Someone named Jones may deny that the God of the Bible exists. He may even be foolish enough to believe that he has no god at all. But perceptive people will readily observe that there is something in life that functions as an object of ultimate concern for Jones.[16] It may be sex or money; or perhaps something as noble as love for his family or the poor. As John Calvin observed, every human being is incurably religious. It is our nature to give ourselves wholeheartedly and unreservedly to something, even if on occasion that something may be nothing more than the betterment of self. But whatever that object of ultimate concern is for us, that will be our god. For this reason, genuine atheists do not exist. Instead, we find those who adore or worship things or ideals in place of the one true

[14]There is no need to complicate the discussion by detailing the many divisions that exist within most of the world's major religions.

[15]A dualistic system teaches the existence of two supreme beings; an example would be the ancient position known as Manichaeism. A polytheistic religion believes in many gods while a pantheistic system tends to regard all of reality as divine in some sense.

[16]It is helpful in this regard to distinguish between a concern and an *ultimate* concern. We all care about many things: love of family, the condition of one's home, taxes, war and peace, the scores of last night's baseball games, and so on. But for each of us, there can be only one ultimate concern, something so important that we are willing, at the moment, to sacrifice almost anything for it. Also for the record, objects of ultimate concern change over time; sometimes they change very quickly for certain people.

God. All such people fall under the judgment implicit in the First Commandment (Ex. 20:3).

Ultimate Reality

A worldview also includes beliefs about ultimate reality, a subject often discussed under the term *metaphysics*. In the philosophical systems of thinkers like Plato and Aristotle, metaphysics often becomes a complex and mysterious subject.[17] But a person's worldview need not be complicated in order for it to include metaphysical beliefs. Those beliefs include answers to such questions as these: What is the relationship between God and the universe? Is the existence of the universe a brute fact? Is the universe eternal? Did an eternal, personal, omnipotent God create the world? Are God and the world coeternal and interdependent?[18] Is the world best understood in a mechanistic (that is, nonpurposeful) way? Or is there a purpose in the universe? What is the ultimate nature of the universe? Is the cosmos ultimately material or spiritual or something else? Is the universe a self-enclosed system in the sense that everything that happens is caused by (and thus explained by) other events within the system? Or can a supernatural reality (a being beyond the natural order) act causally within nature? Are miracles possible?

Though many of these questions never occur to some people, it is likely that anyone reading this book has thought about most of them and holds beliefs about some of them.

[17]For a simple introduction to the thought of Plato and Aristotle, see my *The Gospel and the Greeks*, chap. 2.

[18]Advocates of what is known as process theology answer this question in the affirmative. For a detailed analysis of this increasingly influential position, see Ronald Nash, ed., *Process Theology* (Grand Rapids: Baker, 1987). Also relevant is my *The Concept of God* (Grand Rapids: Zondervan, 1983).

Knowledge

A third component of any worldview is one's view of knowledge. Even people not given to philosophic pursuits hold beliefs on this subject. The easiest way to see this is simply to ask whether they believe that knowledge about the world is possible. Regardless of their answer, their reply will identify one element of their epistemology. Other questions include the following: Can we trust our senses? What are the proper roles of reason and sense experience in knowledge? Do we apprehend our own states of consciousness in some way other than reason and sense experience? Are our intuitions of our own states of consciousness more dependable than our perceptions of the external world? Is truth relative, or must truth be the same for all rational beings? What is the relationship between religious faith and reason? Is the scientific method the only (or perhaps the best) method of knowledge? Is knowledge about God possible? If so, how? Can God reveal himself to human beings? Can God reveal information to human beings?[19] Even though few of us think about questions like these while watching a baseball game (or, indeed, during any normal daily activity), all that is usually required to elicit an opinion is to ask the question.

Ethics

Most people are more aware of the ethical component of their worldview than of their beliefs about metaphysics and epistemology. We make moral judgments about the conduct of individuals (ourselves and others) and about nations. The kinds of ethical beliefs that are important in this context, however, are more basic than moral judgments about single actions. It is one thing to say that an action of a human being like Saddam Hussein or of a nation like Iraq is

[19]My answers to many of these questions can be found in my *The Word of God and the Mind of Man*.

morally wrong. But ethics as a worldview factor is more concerned with the question of *why* that action is wrong. Are there moral laws that govern human conduct? What are they? Are these moral laws the same for all human beings? Is morality totally subjective (like our taste for spinach), or is there an objective dimension to moral laws that means their truth is independent of our preferences and desires? Are the moral laws discovered (in a way more or less similar to the way we discover that seven times seven equals forty-nine), or are they constructed by human beings (in a way more or less similar to what we call a society's mores)? Is morality relative to individuals or to cultures or to historical periods? Does it make sense to say that the same action may be right for people in one culture or historical epoch and wrong for others? Or does morality transcend cultural, historical, and individual boundaries?[20]

Humankind

Every worldview includes a number of important beliefs about human beings. Examples include the following: Are human beings free, or are they merely pawns of deterministic forces? Or is there an alternative to these extremes? Are human beings only bodies or material beings? Or were all the religious and philosophical thinkers correct who talked about the human soul or who distinguished the mind from the body? If they were right in some sense, what is the human soul or mind, and how is it related to the body? Does physical death end the existence of the human person? Or is there conscious, personal survival after death? Are there rewards and punishment after death? Are Christian teachings about heaven and hell correct?

[20]A well-known, popularly written set of answers to many of these questions can be found in Part 1 of C. S. Lewis's *Mere Christianity* (New York: Macmillan, 1960).

Additional Questions

Are the five points just noted the *only* components of what may properly be called a worldview? While the correct answer is no, consciously held beliefs about other elements of a worldview appear to be less common. I will comment on two.

1. A person's worldview may also include a set of ideals that lays out how he or she thinks things should be. These ideals produce a gap between the way things are and the way they ought to be.[21] Regardless of the actual conditions that may exist in one's life or society, one may have a vision or picture of how things ought to be different. Perhaps there should be less stupidity or corruption among politicians; perhaps I should lose my temper less often; perhaps my eating habits should be different; perhaps there should be more justice or less poverty in the world. These ideals apply to many different aspects of human existence: family, church, school, business, government. Things can always be better than they are.

2. A well-formed worldview may also contain an explanation for the disparity between the way things are and they way they ought to be. Marxists, for example, are prone to blame what they see as problems on the institutions of capitalism. Christianity attributes the discrepancy between the ideal and actual existence to the pervasiveness of sin.

An Important Qualification

Because my purpose thus far has been to make a complicated subject as clear as possible, I've been forced to oversimplify some things. This is a good time to make an

---

[21]It is clear that this set of ideals will be a combined function of those elements of a worldview already noted. Moreover, consciousness of one's major beliefs about God, reality, knowledge, ethics, and humankind would seem to be a necessary condition for an awareness of more developed worldview components.

important qualification. I do not want to suggest that adherents of the same general worldview will necessarily agree on every issue. Any account of worldviews that implies total unanimity is grossly mistaken. Even Christians who share beliefs on all essential issues may disagree on other important points. They may understand the relationship between human freedom and the sovereignty of God in different ways. They may disagree over how a revealed law of God applies to a twentieth-century situation. They may squabble publicly over complex issues like national defense, capital punishment, and the welfare state, to say nothing about the issues that divide Christendom into different denominations.

Do these manifold and important disagreements undercut the case I've been making about the nature of the Christian worldview? Not at all. A careful study of these disagreements will reveal that they are differences within a broader family of beliefs. When a Christian argues with another Christian over any issue, one way he justifies his positions and tries to persuade the other is to show that his view is more consistent with basic tenets of the Christian worldview.[22]

However, it is also important to recognize that disagreement over essential Christian beliefs should result in the disputant's being regarded as one who has left the former family of beliefs, however much he or she desires to continue to use the old label. For example, many religious liberals in the West continue to use the Christian label for views that are clearly inconsistent with the beliefs of historic Christianity. Whether they deny the Trinity or the personality of God or the doctrine of creation or the fact of human depravity or the doctrine of salvation by grace, they make clear that the religious system they espouse is totally different from what has traditionally been meant by *Christianity*. A religion without the incarnate, crucified, and

---

[22]For examples of this, see my *Social Justice and the Christian Church* (Lanham, Md.: University Press of America, 1990) and my *Poverty and Wealth* (Dallas: Probe Books, 1992).

risen Son of God may be an expression of some faith, but it certainly is not the *Christian* religion. Much confusion would be avoided if we could find a way to get people to use important labels like Christianity in a way that is faithful to their historic meaning. Since this is not going to happen, we will have to live with the confusion or find other ways to make careful distinctions.

CONCLUSION

Whether we know it or not—whether we like it or not—each of us has a worldview. These worldviews function as interpretive conceptual schemes to explain why we "see" the world as we do, why we often think and act as we do. Competing worldviews often come into conflict. These clashes may be as innocuous as a simple argument between people or as serious as a war between nations. It is important, therefore, for us to understand that competing worldviews are the fundamental cause of our disagreements.

Worldviews are double-edged swords. An inadequate conceptual scheme can, like improper eyeglasses, hinder our efforts to understand God, the world, and ourselves. The right conceptual scheme can suddenly bring everything into focus. But the choices among competing worldviews involve a number of difficult questions. For one thing, we must always contend with the ever-present possibility of nontheoretical factors adversely affecting our thinking. For another, it is difficult to be sure which criteria or tests should be used in choosing among worldviews.☐

Chapter 2

The Christian Worldview

Now that we understand Christian theism is a worldview, the next step is to grasp a brief outline of its content.

GOD

The Christian worldview is theistic in the sense that it believes in the existence of one supremely powerful and personal God. Theism differs from polytheism in its affirmation that there is only one God (Deut. 6:4). It parts company with the various forms of pantheism by insisting that God is personal and must not be confused with the world that is his creation. Theism must also be distinguished from panentheism, the position that regards the world as an eternal being that God needs in much the same way a human soul needs a body. Theists also reject panentheistic attempts to limit God's power and knowledge, which have the effect of making the God of panentheism a finite being.[1] Other important attributes of God,

[1]For a fuller discussion, see Ronald Nash, ed., *Process Theology.* Panentheism can be thought of as a position somewhere between theism's belief in a personal, almighty, all-knowing God and the impersonal god of pantheism that is identical in some way with nature or the world order. While the god of panentheism is not identical with the world, this god and

such as his holiness, justice, and love are described in Scripture.

Historical Christian theism is also trinitarian. The doctrine of the Trinity reflects the Christian conviction that the Father, the Son, and the Holy Spirit are three distinct centers of consciousness sharing fully in the one divine nature and in the activities of the other persons of the Trinity. An important corollary of the doctrine is the Christian conviction that Jesus Christ is both fully God and fully man.[2] Christians use the word *incarnation* to express their belief that the birth of Jesus Christ marked the entrance of the eternal and divine Son of God into the human race.

ULTIMATE REALITY

The Bible begins with the words, "In the beginning God created the heavens and the earth." Many early Christian thinkers found it important to draw out certain implications of the biblical view of God and stipulate that God created the world *ex nihilo* (from nothing), which is an important metaphysical tenet of the Christian worldview. This was necessary, they believed, to show the contrast between the Christian understanding of Creation and an account of the world's origin found in Plato's philosophy, a view held by a number of intellectuals in the early centuries of the Christian church.[3]

Plato had suggested that a godlike being, the Crafts-man, had brought the world into being by fashioning an

the world necessarily co-exist eternally. Another basic feature of panentheism is the denial of the view that God can act as an efficient cause, a belief that precludes any belief in either creation or in such miracles as the Incarnation or the Resurrection.

[2]It is important for Christians to realize that the belief that Jesus is fully God and fully man does not involve them in a logical contradiction. Critics of Christianity like to deceive people into thinking that this Christian claim is similar to believing that something is a square circle. It is not.

[3]For more on this, see my *The Gospel and the Greeks*.

eternal stuff or matter after the pattern of eternal ideas that existed independently of the Craftsman. Moreover, this creative activity took place in a space-time receptacle or box that also existed independently of the Craftsman. Such early Christian thinkers as Augustine wanted the world to know that the Christian God and the Christian view of Creation differed totally from this platonic picture. Plato's god (if indeed that is an appropriate word for his Craftsman) was not the infinite, all-powerful, and sovereign God of the Christian Scriptures. Plato's god was finite and limited. In the Christian account of Creation, nothing existed prior to Creation except God. There was no time or space; there was no preexisting matter. Everything else that exists besides God depends totally upon God for its existence. If God did not exist, the world would not exist. The cosmos is not eternal, self-sufficient, or self-explanatory. It was freely created by God.

The existence of the world, therefore, is not a brute fact; nor is the world a purposeless machine. The world exists as the result of a free decision to create by a God who is eternal, transcendent, spiritual (that is, nonmaterial), omnipotent, omniscient, omnibenevolent, loving, and personal. Because there is a God-ordained order to the creation, human beings can discover that order. It is this order that makes science possible; it is this order that scientists attempt to capture in their laws.

The Christian worldview should be distinguished from any version of deism. This theory dared to suggest that although God created the world, he absents himself from the creation and allows it to run on its own. This view and several twentieth-century varieties seem to present the picture of a God (or god) who is incapable of acting causally within nature.[4] While no informed Christian will argue

---

[4]This certainly appears to have been the view of such twentieth-century theologians as Paul Tillich and Rudolf Bultmann. While the term *naturalism* will be explained later, there is some justification for describing thinkers like Tillich and Bultmann as religious naturalists. They may

with the assured results of such sciences as physics, biology, and geology, the Christian worldview insists that divine activities such as miracles, revelation, and providence remain possible.

KNOWLEDGE

The study of epistemology can quickly involve one in fairly sticky problems. In fact, one should admit that on many epistemological issues (for example, the dispute between rationalists and empiricists)[5] a wide variety of options seems to be consistent with other aspects of the Christian worldview. But there do seem to be limits to this tolerance. For example, the Christian worldview is clearly incompatible with universal skepticism, the self-defeating claim that no knowledge about anything is attainable. The fact that this kind of skepticism self-destructs becomes clear whenever one asks such a skeptic whether he knows that knowledge is unattainable.

It also seems obvious that a well-formed Christian worldview will exclude views suggesting that humans cannot attain knowledge about God. Christianity clearly proclaims that God has revealed information about himself.[6] Nor will an informed Christian deny the importance of the senses in supplying information about the world. As St. Augustine observed, the Christian "believes also the evidence of the senses which the mind uses by aid of the body; for if one who trusts his senses is sometimes deceived, he is more wretchedly deceived who fancies he should never trust them."[7] In his own theory of knowledge,

have believed in God, but their God was effectively precluded from any providential or miraculous activity within the natural order.

[5]For the reader unfamiliar with these terms, an empiricist is a person who believes that all human knowledge can be traced back to bodily experience. A rationalist, on the other hand, believes that some human knowledge can originate in something other than sense experience.

[6]I defend this claim in *The Word of God and the Mind of Man*.

[7]Augustine, *City of God*, trans. Marcus Dods (New York: Modern Library, 1950), 19.18.

Augustine was a rationalist in the sense that he gave priority to reason over sense experience. Augustine probably had a good theological reason for defending the general reliability of sense experience. He undoubtedly realized that many claims made in the Bible depended upon eyewitness testimony. If the senses are completely unreliable, we cannot trust the reports of witnesses who say that they heard Jesus teach or saw him die or saw him alive three days after the Crucifixion. If the experiences of those who saw and heard a risen Christ were necessarily deceptive and unreliable, an important truth of the Christian faith is compromised.

In recent Christian writings about the theory of knowledge, philosophers apparently operating on different tracks have found agreement on an important point. In the case of my own track (a kind of Christian rationalism that received its first formulation in the writings of St. Augustine), it is a mistake to accept an extreme form of empiricism that claims *all* human knowledge rises from sense experience. Older advocates of this empiricism used to illustrate their basic claim by arguing that the human mind at birth is like a *tabula rasa*, a blank tablet. At birth, the human mind is like a totally clean blackboard; absolutely nothing is written on it. In other words, human beings are born with no innate ideas or knowledge. As the human being grows and develops, the senses supply the mind with an ever-increasing stock of information. All human knowledge results, in this model, from what the mind does with ideas supplied through the senses—the basic building blocks of knowledge.

My alternative to this extreme kind of empiricism can be summarized in the claim that *some* human knowledge does not rise from sense experience.[8] As many philosophers have noted, human knowledge of the sensible world is possible because human beings bring certain ideas, catego-

---

[8]I consciously reject an extreme type of rationalism that claims *no* human knowledge rises from sense experience. Plato held this latter view. But as explained earlier, Augustine did not; nor do I.

ries, and dispositions to their experience of the world. The impotence of empiricism is especially evident in the case of human knowledge of universal and necessary truth. Many things in the world could have been otherwise. The typewriter I am using at this moment happens to be brown, but it could have been red. Whether it is brown or not is a purely contingent feature of reality. Regardless of the color my typewriter happens to be, it could have been colored differently. But it is *necessarily* the case that my typewriter could not have been brown all over and red (or any other color) all over at the same time and in the same sense. The necessary truth that my typewriter is brown all over and not at the same time red all over cannot be a function of sense experience. Sense experience may be able to report what is fact at a particular time. But sense experience is incapable of grasping what *must* be the case *at all times*. The notions of necessity and universality can never be derived from our experience. Rather, they are notions (among others) that we bring to sense experience and use in making judgments about reality.

How do we account for the human possession of these categories of thought or innate ideas or dispositions that play such an indispensable role in human knowledge? According to a long and honored philosophical tradition that includes Augustine, Descartes, and Leibniz, human beings have these innate ideas, dispositions, and categories of thought by virtue of their creation by God. In fact, this may well be part of what is meant by the phrase *the image of God*.[9] After all (Christians believe), God created the world. It is reasonable to assume that he created humans in such a way as to make them capable of attaining knowledge of his creation. To go even further, it is reasonable to believe that he endowed the human mind with the ability to attain knowledge of himself.

[9] I have explored the roots of this theory in the writings of St. Augustine in my book *The Light of the Mind: St. Augustine's Theory of Knowledge* (Lexington, Ky.: University Press of Kentucky, 1969). This work is then brought up to date in *The Word of God and the Mind of Man*.

Philosopher Alvin Plantinga has noted an important similarity between the role that God-given categories and dispositions play in human knowledge and what Reformed thinkers like John Calvin said about belief in God.

> Reformed Theologians such as Calvin . . . have held that God has implanted in us a tendency . . . to accept belief in God under certain conditions. Calvin speaks, in this connection, of a "sense of deity inscribed in the hearts of all." Just as we have a natural tendency to form perceptual beliefs under certain conditions, so says Calvin, we have a natural tendency to form such beliefs as *God is speaking to me* and *God has created all this* or *God disapproves of what I've done* under certainly widely realized conditions.[10]

Plantinga shows no reluctance to describe the idea of God as "innate," that is, present in the mind from birth, not derived from experience.

These are complex issues. But it is clear that the Christian worldview is no ally of skepticism. Human beings can know God's creation; they are also capable of attaining knowledge about God. Nor should this surprise anyone. It is exactly what we should have expected.

ETHICS

The fact that all human beings carry the image of God (another of Christianity's claims about human nature) explains why human beings are creatures capable of reasoning, love, and God-consciousness; it also explains why we are moral creatures. Of course, sin (yet another of Christianity's important presuppositions about human beings) has distorted the image of God and explains why humans turn

---

[10]Alvin Plantinga, "Self-Profile," in *Alvin Plantinga*, ed. James E. Tomberlin and Peter van Inwagen (Boston: D. Reidel, 1985), 63, 64. Plantinga's quote comes from Calvin's *Institutes of the Christian Religion*, bk. 1, chap. 3, 43–44.

away from God and the moral law; why we sometimes go wrong with regard to our emotions, conduct, and thinking.

Because of the image of God, we should expect to find that the ethical recommendations of the Christian worldview reflect what all of us at the deepest levels of our moral being know to be true. As C. S. Lewis pointed out,

> Christ did not come to preach any brand new morality. . . . Really great moral teachers never do introduce new moralities; it is quacks and cranks who do that. . . . The real job of every moral teacher is to keep on bringing us back, time after time, to the old simple principles which we are all so anxious not to see.[11]

When one examines the moralities of different cultures and religions, certain differences do stand out. But Lewis was more impressed by the basic, underlying similarities:

> Think of a country where people were admired for running away in battle, or where a man felt proud of doublecrossing all the people who had been kindest to him. You might just as well try to imagine a country where two and two made five. Men have differed as regards what people you ought to be unselfish to— whether it was only your own family, or your fellow countrymen, or everyone. But they have always agreed that you ought not to put yourself first. Selfishness has never been admired.[12]

According to the Christian worldview, God is the ground of the laws that govern the physical universe and that make possible the order of the cosmos. God is also the ground of the moral laws that ought to govern human behavior and that make possible order between humans and within humans.[13]

[11]Lewis, *Mere Christianity*, 78.
[12]Ibid., 19.
[13]Each of the areas dealing with God, ultimate reality, knowledge, ethics, and humankind includes its share of important but different questions that cannot be pursued in this study. One such problem in ethics is the precise relationship between God and morality. For some technical discussions of the topic, see Philip L. Quinn, *Divine Commands and*

Christian theism insists on the existence of universal moral laws. In other words, the laws must apply to all humans, regardless of when or where they have lived. They must also be objective in the sense that their truth is independent of human preference and desire.

Much confusion surrounding Christian ethics results from a failure to observe the important distinction between principles and rules. Let us define moral principles as more *general* moral prescriptions, general in the sense that they cover a large number of instances. Moral rules, on the other hand, will be regarded as more *specific* moral prescriptions that are, in fact, applications of principles to more concrete situations.

The difference between principles and rules has advantages and disadvantages. One advantage of moral principles is the fact that they are less subject to change. Because of the larger number of instances where they are applicable, they possess a greater degree of universality. One disadvantage of any moral principle is its vagueness. Because principles cover so many situations, it is often difficult to know exactly when a particular principle applies. Rules, however, have the advantage of being much more specific. Their problem is their changeableness. Because they are so closely tied to specific situations, changes in circumstances usually require changes in the appropriate rule. For example, St. Paul warned the Christian women of Corinth not to worship with their heads uncovered. Some Christians have mistakenly regarded Paul's advice as a moral principle that should be observed by Christian women in every culture at all times. But a study of the conditions that prevailed in ancient Corinth reveals that the city's prostitutes identified themselves to their prospective customers by keeping their heads uncovered. In the light of this, it seems likely that Paul's advice was not a moral principle intended to apply to

Moral Requirements (Oxford: Clarendon Press, 1978), and Robert Merrihew Adams, "A Modified Divine Command Theory of Ethical Wrongness" in *Religion and Morality*, Gene Outka and John P. Reeder, Jr., eds. (Garden City, N. Y.: Anchor Press, Doubleday, 1973).

Christians of all generations but a rule that applied only to the specific situation of the Christian women of Corinth and to other women in similar situations.[14]

The following chart may help clarify the points of the last paragraph:

	Advantage	Disadvantage
Principles	Universal	Vague
Rules	Specific	Situational

I recognize that the distinction I am drawing here suffers from impreciseness. This is due in part to the fact that the difference between principles and rules is sometimes relative. That is, Scripture actually presents a hierarchy of moral prescriptions beginning at the most general level with the duty to love. This duty to love is then further broken down into the duties to love God and love people (Matt. 22:37–40), and then still further into the more specific duties of the Decalogue (Rom. 13:9–10). And, of course, the still more specific duties spelled out in the New Testament, such as the prohibition against the lustful look and hatred, are further specifications of the Ten Commandments (Matt. 5:21–30). The distinction between principles and rules suggests that whenever you have two scriptural injunctions, where a more specific command is derived from the more general, you can regard the more specific injunction as the rule and the other as the principle. It is possible to read 1 Corinthians 13 in this way. First, Paul proposes love as a moral duty binding on all. Then he proceeds to provide more specific rules about how a loving

[14]Even if my particular interpretation of 1 Corinthians 11 is challenged, my point can be made in terms of other New Testament passages. See, for example, Paul's remarks in Romans 14 concerning Christians eating meat that had been offered to pagan gods.

person will behave; for example, he will be kind and patient.

Based on our distinction between principles and rules plus a careful study of the New Testament, we can draw several conclusions:

(1) The New Testament gave first-century Christians plenty of rules. But, of course, the rules cover situations that may no longer confront twentieth-century Christians, such as Paul's injunction against eating meat offered to idols.

(2) The New Testament does not provide twentieth-century Christians with any large number of rules regarding *our* specific situations. The reason is obvious. The rules were given to cover first-century situations. A first-century book that attempted to give moral rules to cover specific twentieth-century situations would have become unintelligible or irrelevant to readers in the intervening nineteen hundred years. What moral help could the first-century Christians in Rome or Ephesus have derived from such a moral rule as "thou shalt not make a first strike with nuclear weapons" or "it is wrong to use cocaine"?

(3) At the same time, some of the New Testament rules apply to situations that have existed throughout time. Passages dealing with acts of hating, stealing, lying, and the like continue to be relevant because the acts are similar.

(4) But often what many people miss is the importance of searching out the moral *principles* behind the New Testament rules. These principles are equally binding on humans of all generations. A careful consideration of the Bible's first-century rules enables us to infer the more general principles behind them, principles that apply to us today. It may be unimportant today whether Christian women keep their heads covered, but it

is important that they avoid provocative dress and behavior. Though few Christians in our generation are bothered by pagan butchers who have offered their wares as a sacrifice to a false god, we can profit from the principle that we should do nothing that causes a spiritually weaker person to stumble.[15]

While a properly formed Christian worldview allows a great deal of leeway regarding the positions sincere Christians may take on many of the tough problems that rise in the formulation of an ethical theory, informed Christians will have to reject certain views. One such view is the position called situation ethics, which asserts that Christian ethics imposes no duty other than the duty to love. In determining what he should do, the situationist declares, the Christian should face the moral situation and ask himself what the loving thing to do is in this particular case. No rules or principles prescribe how love will act. Indeed, each loving individual is free to act in any way he thinks is consistent with love as he understands it. The point to situation ethics is, then, that Christian ethics provides no universal principles and no specific rules. Nothing is intrinsically good except love; nothing intrinsically bad except nonlove. One can never prescribe in advance what a Christian should or should not do. Depending on the situation, love may find it necessary to lie, to steal, even presumably to fornicate, to blaspheme, and to worship false gods. The only absolute is love.

A proper response to situation ethics will begin by pointing out that love is insufficient in itself to provide moral guidance for each and every moral action. Love

---

[15]Another qualification may help some readers. I am not suggesting that Scripture presents us with a casuistic system of morality in which specific moral duties can always be deduced from more general moral statements. Casuistry always leads to a type of legalism that is condemned by Scripture. But I do think a recognition of a biblical hierarchy of rules and principles can help us determine our duty.

requires the further specification of principles or rules that suggest the proper ways in which love should be manifested. Because human beings are fallen creatures whose judgments on moral matters may be affected by moral weakness, love needs guidance from divinely revealed moral truth. Fortunately, Christians believe, this content is provided in the moral principles revealed in Scripture.

In spite of all this, life often confronts us with ambiguous moral situations in which even the most sincere among us may agonize over what to do. At times we simply do not know enough about ourselves, the situation, or the moral principle that applies to be sure we are doing the right thing. As many of us also know, weakness of will can hinder moral decision making.

In the unambiguous situations of life, Scripture teaches, God judges us in terms of our obedience to his revealed moral law. But how does God judge us in the more ambiguous situations where the precise nature of our duty is unclear? God looks upon the heart, Scripture advises. We are judged if we break God's commandments. This is certain. But in those cases where we may not know which commandment applies or where we may have incomplete knowledge of the situation, God's judgment will take into account not merely the rightness of the consequences of our act (something that we ourselves are often unable to determine in ambiguous situations) but the goodness of our intentions.

HUMANKIND

William J. Abraham provides us with an introduction to the complex subject of what the Christian worldview teaches about human beings:

> Human beings are made in the image of God, and their fate depends on their relationship with God. They are free to respond to or reject God and they will be judged in accordance with how they respond to him. This

46

judgment begins now but finally takes place beyond death in a life to come. Christians furthermore offer a diagnosis of what is wrong with the world. Fundamentally, they say, our problems are spiritual: we need to be made anew by God. Human beings have misused their freedom; they are in a state of rebellion against God; they are sinners. These conclusions lead to a set of solutions to this ill. As one might expect, the fundamental solution is again spiritual. . . . [I]n Jesus of Nazareth God has intervened to save and remake mankind. Each individual needs to respond to this and to become part of Christ's body, the church, where they are to grow in grace and become more like Christ. This in turn generates a certain vision of the future. In the coming of Jesus, God has inaugurated his kingdom, but it will be consummated at some unspecified time in the future when Christ returns.[16]

What a paradox human beings are! The only bearers of the image of God on this planet are also capable of the most heinous acts. As Pascal put it, "What a freak, what a monster, what a chaos, what a subject of contradiction, what a marvel! Judge of all things, and imbecile earthworm; possessor of the truth, and sink of uncertainty and error; glory and rubbish of the universe."[17] In another passage, Pascal wrote,

Man is but a reed, the weakest in nature, but he is a thinking reed. The whole universe need not arm itself to crush him; a vapor, a drop of water is enough to kill him. But even though the universe should crush him, man would still be nobler than what kills him since he knows that he dies, and the advantage that the universe has over him, the universe knows nothing of it.[18]

[16]Abraham, *An Introduction to the Philosophy of Religion* (Englewood Cliffs, N.J.: Prentice-Hall, 1985), 104–5.
[17]Blaise Pascal, *Selections from The Thoughts*, trans. Arthur H. Beattie (New York: Appleton-Century-Crofts, 1965), 68.
[18]Ibid., 30.

47

The essential paradox here—the greatness and the misery of humankind—flows out of two important truths. God created humans as the apex of his creation; our chief end, in the words of the Westminster Catechism, is to glorify God and enjoy him forever. But each human being is fallen, is in rebellion against the God who created him and loves him.

Christianity simply will not make sense to people who fail to understand and appreciate the Christian doctrine of sin. Every human being lives in a condition of sin and alienation from his or her Creator. Each has sinned and fallen short of God's standard (Rom. 3:23). As John Stott counsels, sin "is not a convenient invention of parsons to keep them in their job; it is a fact of human experience."[19] The sin that separates us from God and enslaves us

> is more than an unfortunate outward act of habit; it is a deep-seated inward corruption. In fact, the sins we commit are merely outward and visible manifestations of this inward and invisible malady, the symptoms of a moral disease. . . . Because sin is an inward corruption of human nature we are in bondage. It is not so much certain acts or habits which enslave us, but rather the evil infection from which these spring.[20]

In the writings of the nineteenth-century Christian writer Søren Kierkegaard, human alienation from God often rises to the surface in the form of moods like despair. As Kierkegaard described it in his technical way, two aspects of human existence (the finite/temporal and the infinite/eternal) compete for dominance in the life of every human being. Unless a person succeeds in getting these two dimensions into proper relation and manages somehow to unify them, he or she will never really be a self. Apart from God, each human being is a divided self.

Clearly, each of us is finite in many respects. We are limited and restricted by our bodies, our circumstances, our

[19]John Stott, *Basic Christianity* (Grand Rapids: Eerdmans, 1967), 61.
[20]Ibid., 75, 76.

surroundings, our weakness of will. A constant and unavoidable reminder of the limitations of our existence is
provided by death—the actual death of others and the
realization of the inevitability of our own death. But there
is also another side to our existence, a side that takes on
dimensions of infinity or eternity. For one thing, our desires
seem to transcend the finite limitations of our bodies. We
always desire more than we have; we always want more
than we can possibly achieve. No matter what we have
accomplished or attained in the way of fame, fortune,
pleasure, or happiness, we want more. In a very real sense,
our appetites are never satisfied. This is not to ignore times
when thoroughly satiated individuals pause, momentarily
content with the most recent satisfaction of their desires.
But the contentment soon disappears, and they are back on
the trail, searching for more.

The frustration resulting from the human inability
ultimately to satisfy all desires is just one manifestation of
the tension between the finite and infinite poles of our
being. Another example is the tendency of many to seek
escape from reality through flights of fantasy. Rather than
confront the truth about the closed frontiers of their
existence, many people prefer to live in a world of dreams
and illusions. In spite of their age, such people suffer from
lifelong immaturity. They never really grow up.

Because most people never succeed in pulling the
finite and infinite sides of their being together, they go
through life suffering the spiritual and emotional consequences of being divided selves. Despair is one result of the
failure to put the various parts of one's life together.
Despair is essentially enthusiasm that has gone astray, that
has lost its bearings; it is a zeal for things that either
disappear when they are most wanted or fail to deliver all
that they seem to promise. If, in a person's unconscious, he
or she begins to feel that all the deepest yearnings of the
soul will eventually end up unsatisfied, the onset of despair
makes a kind of perverse sense. It is perfectly understandable how one's unconscious, under these conditions, might

react by repressing enthusiasm, thus producing the mood of despair.

The victim of moods like despair is frequently unaware of the problem. Kierkegaard clearly thought that despair is often unconscious. The individual senses dimly that something is wrong, without ever being able to put a finger on it. The great extent to which despair functions in human lives below the level of consciousness may be one more result of the refusal of many people to face the truth about themselves and their world. The truly unhappy person who mistakenly believes himself or herself happy tends to regard as an enemy everyone who threatens that illusion.

Moods like despair are also indications that the major source of human trouble lies within, not in external circumstances. Consider the contrast in the writings of St. Paul between *sins*, the overt acts, and *sin*, the depraved nature within. Human beings are not self-sufficient; we cannot cure ourselves. We can become selves, we can grow up and develop into complete human beings only through a proper relationship with God. The finite and infinite must be joined from without, by God himself. Despair is only one symptom of estrangement from God and consequently from the self. Divided selves can achieve the unity of selfhood only in a faith-relationship with God.

One final aspect of Kierkegaard's analysis deserves attention. Moods like despair indicate

that people are not wholly or ultimately made for this world. There is "something eternal" in us. We are to find the fulfillment of our passion for meaning and security, which is expressed in a distorted way by our typical immersion in these worldly projects, in a realm which is not subject to disappearance. A human being is not an absurdity, a futile passion, doomed either to repression or the most poignant unhappiness. He is, rather, a wayward child of God, whose restlessness and anxiety and despair can and should drive him into the arms of his Father. His despair is indeed a sickness, but it is curable when he finds his true home.[21]

The eternal factor that God has implanted within leaves all of us ultimately frustrated, unhappy, and restless until we finally enter into his rest. As Augustine put it, God has made us for himself, and our hearts are restless until they rest in him. Human beings are driven to seek an eternal peace, in which everything will finally be in its proper place, in which perfect order both in the world and in the soul will be attained. Despair may be one way God informs us that we are to look beyond ourselves for our ultimate peace. It is one of several moods and affective states that ought to remind alert people that we should know better than to think that our highest good can be found in this life.

The Christian worldview recognizes the human need for forgiveness and redemption and stresses that the blessings of salvation are possible because of Jesus' death and resurrection. Christ's redemptive work is the basis of human salvation. But human beings are required to repent of sins (be sorry for and turn from sins) and believe. Accepting Christ as one's Lord and Savior brings about a new birth, a new heart, a new relationship with God, and a new power to live.[22] Christian conversion does not suddenly make the new Christian perfect. But the Christian has God's nature and Spirit within and is called to live a particular kind of life in obedience to God's will. Finally, the Christian worldview teaches that physical death is not the end of personal existence.

CHRISTIANITY'S "TOUCHSTONE PROPOSITION"

Even my short outline of the Christian worldview may seem involved to some readers. Is it possible to boil

[21]Robert C. Roberts, "The Transparency of Faith," *The Reformed Journal* (June 1979), 11.
[22]See John 3:3–21; Galatians 2:20, Hebrews 8:10–12; and 1 John 3:1–2.

everything down to one proposition? In this connection, William Halverson makes an interesting observation:

> At the center of every worldview is what might be called the "touchstone proposition" of that worldview, a proposition that is held to be *the* fundamental truth about reality and serves as a criterion to determine which other propositions may or may not count as candidates for belief. If a given proposition *P* is seen to be inconsistent with the touchstone proposition or one's worldview, then so long as one holds that worldview, proposition *P* must be regarded as false.[23]

There is value in seeing how Halverson's suggestion applies to what has already been said about the Christian worldview. Does one touchstone proposition or control belief or ultimate presupposition that is the fundamental truth of this particular worldview also serve as the test that any belief must pass before it can be included as part of the worldview?

One proposition that may fill the bill is the following: "Human beings and the universe in which they reside are the creation of the God who has revealed himself in Scripture."[24] The basic presupposition of the Christian worldview is the existence of God revealed in Scripture.

This linkage between God and the Scripture is proper. It is true, naturally, that this particular touchstone proposition allows the Christian ready access to all that Scripture says about God, the world, and humankind. While that is certainly an advantage, it is hardly an unfair advantage. What would be both unwise and unfair would be any attempt to separate the Christian God from his self-disclosure. As Carl F. H. Henry points out, God is not "a nameless spirit awaiting post-mortem examination in some theological morgue. He is a very particular and specific

[23]William H. Halverson, *A Concise Introduction to Philosophy*, 3d. ed. (New York: Random House, 1976), 384.
[24]By Scripture, I mean of course the canonical books of the Old and New Testaments.

divinity, known from the beginning solely on the basis of his works and self-declaration as the one living God."[25]

Any final decision regarding the existence of the Christian God and the truth of the Christian worldview will necessarily involve decisions about issues related to the Christian Scriptures. Since details of that worldview flow from the Christian's ultimate authority, the Bible, any negative reaction to one will likely produce a negative reaction to the other. Of course, to turn the coin over, a positive evaluation of one side of this equation should bear positively on the other. The Christian cannot pretend that his worldview was formulated in a revelational vacuum.

CONCLUSION

While all mature, thinking persons have a worldview, many of them are unaware of the fact. People often evidence great difficulty attaining consciousness of key elements of their worldview. Most of us know individuals who seldom think deeply enough to ask the right questions about God, metaphysics, epistemology, ethics, and humankind. As I have said, one of the important tasks for philosophers, theologians, and, indeed, for anyone interested in helping people in this important matter, is first to get people to realize that they do have a conceptual system. The second step is to help people get a clearer fix on the content of their worldview. What do they believe about the existence and nature of God, about humankind, morality, knowledge, and ultimate reality? The third step is to help people evaluate their worldview and either improve it (by removing inconsistencies and filling in gaps) or replace it with a better worldview. In the next chapter, I will examine recommendations regarding the best or most promising way to go about making a choice among competing worldviews.☐

[25]Carl F. H. Henry, *God, Revelation and Authority*, vol. 2: *God Who Speaks and Shows* (Waco: Word, 1976), 7.

Chapter 3

How To Choose
a Worldview

Since Christian theism is only one of many competing worldviews, on what grounds can people make a reasoned choice among the systems? Which worldview is most likely to be true? What is the best or most promising way to approach this kind of question?

When faced with a choice among competing touchstone propositions of different worldviews, we should choose the one that, when applied to the whole of reality, gives us the most coherent picture of the world. After all, as Gordon C. Clark explains, "If one system can provide plausible solutions to many problems while another leaves too many questions unanswered, if one system tends less to skepticism and gives more meaning to life, if one worldview is consistent while others are self-contradictory, who can deny us, since we must choose, the right to choose the more promising first principle?"[1] The purpose of this chapter is to pursue this general line of thought and fill in many of the necessary details.

[1]Gordon C. Clark, *A Christian View of Men and Things* (Grand Rapids: Eerdmans, 1952), 34.

TESTING A WORLDVIEW

Three major tests should be applied when evaluating worldviews. They are:

The Test of Reason

The Test of Experience

The Test of Practice

THE TEST OF REASON

For entirely too many Christians, reason is seen somehow as an enemy of the Christian faith. I disagree strongly with that widely held but self-destructive thesis.

By the test of reason I mean logic or, to be more specific, the law of noncontradiction. Attempts to define the law of noncontradiction seldom induce much in the way of excitement, but I offer a definition anyway. The law of noncontradiction states that A, which can be anything whatever, cannot be both B and non-B at the same time in the same sense. For example, a proposition cannot be true and false at the same time in the same sense; an object cannot be both round and square; a living being cannot be both a human and a dog at the same time in the same sense.

The presence of a contradiction is always a sign of error. Hence, we have a right to expect a conceptual system to be logically consistent, both in its parts (its individual propositions) and in the whole. A conceptual system is in obvious trouble if it fails to hang together logically.

Logical incoherence can be more or less fatal, depending on whether the contradiction exists among less central beliefs or whether it lies at the very heart of the system. It is because of this second, more serious kind of failing that such systems as skepticism and solipsism self-destruct.

Clark puts his finger on the Achilles' heel of skepticism:

Skepticism is the position that nothing can be demonstrated. And how, we ask, can you demonstrate that nothing can be demonstrated? The skeptic asserts that nothing can be known. In his haste he said that truth was impossible. And is it true that truth is impossible? For, if no proposition is true, then at least one proposition is true—the proposition, namely, that no proposition is true. If truth is impossible, therefore, it follows that we have already attained it.[2]

The skeptic affirms a contradiction, for while he holds that no one can know anything, he is quite certain that he himself *knows* that no one can know anything; or, at least, he *knows* that he doubts that anyone can know anything.

Some philosophers have described such views as being *self-referentially absurd*. What this means is that whenever such a position is applied to itself, the result is nonsense—self-defeating nonsense. Solipsism is another theory that seems to fall into this trap. A solipsist is a person who claims that he alone exists. Nothing else and no one else exists. But then, one must wonder, to whom is the solipsist making this claim? Why would anyone who seriously believes that he is the only being who exists expend such energy in trying to produce arguments supporting his belief?

Because of its importance, and the difficulty that some people have in grasping it, I will comment further in chapter four on the test of reason. For now, I am content to make the point that worldviews should always be submitted to the test of the law of noncontradiction. Inconsistency is always a sign of error. As noted, some philosophical positions or systems seem to self-destruct in the sense that they are internally self-defeating.

Clearly, the charge of inconsistency should be taken seriously. Unless proponents of a worldview can successfully rebut the charge, they ought to regard their system as being terminally ill.

[2]Ibid., 30.

For all its importance, however, the test of logical consistency can never be the only criterion by which we evaluate worldviews. At most, logic can be only a negative test. While the presence of a contradiction will alert us to the presence of error, the absence of contradiction does not guarantee the presence of truth. For that, we need other criteria.

THE TEST OF EXPERIENCE

Worldviews must pass not only the test of reason; they must also satisfy the test of experience. Worldviews should be relevant to what we know about the world and ourselves.

However, an important distinction must be introduced at this point. Certainly the human experience that functions as a test of worldview beliefs includes our experience of the world outside us. It is proper for people to object when a worldview claim conflicts with what we know to be true of the physical universe. This is one reason why no reader of this book believes that the world is flat or that the sun is the center of the universe. It does appear, however, that many who urge objective validation fail to give proper credit to the subjective validation provided by our consciousness of our "inner world."[3] For this reason,

---

[3]My language in this section should not be understood in a way that suggests I view the human being as some kind of "ghost in a machine." Phrases like *outer world, inner world*, and *the world outside us* are simply metaphors that come naturally to all of us who do not, at the moment, happen to be reading a paper to a philosophy seminar. My language is not intended to imply any particular metaphysical theory (for example, an opinion with regard to the mind-body problem) or epistemological view (such as a representative theory of sense-perception). To use a rather fancy term, my language is *phenomenological language*; that is, it describes the way different things appear to us. My experience of my typewriter at this moment is *of* an object that appears to exist outside of and independent of my consciousness or awareness of the typewriter. My consciousness of my own mental states (expressible in propositions like "I am hungry") is *of* something that most people can describe comfortably as belonging to their inner world. As long as the language is understood in a nonliteral way, there is no problem.

my brief account of the test of experience will be divided into two parts: the test of the outer world and the test of the inner world.

The Test of the Outer World

We have a right to expect worldviews to touch base with our experience of the world outside us. They should help us to understand what we perceive.

A number of worldview beliefs fall short of this test. They include the following:

1. God created the world six thousand years ago.
2. Pain and death are illusions.
3. All human beings are innately good.
4. Miracles are impossible.

Fortunately, few Christians today follow the misguided suggestions of some who teach that the world is only six thousand years old. The erroneous computation of biblical chronology that led Archbishop Ussher to this conclusion is now widely rejected. Hence, few Christians have problems understanding coal beds and fossils on this planet or the light from suns millions of light-years away. While a few aging religious modernists and yuppie followers of New Age cults still believe in the inherent goodness of people, Christians and other realistic observers recognize the untaught, unlearned propensity of human beings to sin. And as we will see soon enough, the modern repudiation of miracles is not a conclusion derived from irrefutable evidence but is instead a consequence of a quasi-religious commitment to the worldview known as naturalism.

The inability of the second proposition in my list— the belief that pain and death are illusions—to pass the test of our experience of the outer world is one I think about often because of a sad experience I had many years ago. Many years ago I was employed as an orderly in a New England hospital. One day a Christian Scientist was admitted with terminal cancer. Aware that Christian Science denied the reality of sickness, pain, and death, I wondered why she was there. Then I learned that as the cancer spread and her condition grew desperate, the odor from her diseased flesh became so unbearable her family put her into the hospital to rid the house of the stench. She died within a few days. One can repeat the words "all of this is only an illusion" all one wants. The claims are contradicted by the test of the outer world.

I do not want my position on this particular test misunderstood. Conformity with human observation is not the exclusive test of worldview claims. That should be clear because of what I have already said about reason as a test. I am not an empiricist; that is, I do not believe that all human knowledge begins with sense experience.[4] Nor do I assume that humans are always capable of approaching sense-information in an impersonal and detached way.[5] And I certainly do not believe that proponents of competing worldviews will always interpret the same sense information in the same way. But I do insist on taking the commonsense view that no worldview deserves respect if it ignores or is inconsistent with human experience. I also insist, however, that the human experience we consider when evaluating worldviews be broad enough to include experience of both the outer and the inner worlds.

The Test of the Inner World

As we have seen, worldviews should fit what we know about the external world. But they also need to fit what we know about ourselves. Examples of this second kind of information include the following: I am a being who thinks, hopes, experiences pleasure and pain, believes, desires. I am also a being who is often conscious of right and wrong and who feels guilty and sinful for having failed to do what was

[4] See my *The Word of God and the Mind of Man*, especially chap. 7.
[5] See my *Christian Faith and Historical Understanding* (Dallas: Probe Books, 1984).

right. I am a being who remembers the past, is conscious of the present, and anticipates the future. I can think about things that do not exist. I can plan and then execute my plans. I am able to act intentionally; instead of merely responding to stimuli, I can will to do something and then actually do it. I am a person who loves other human beings. I can empathize with others and share their sorrow and joy. I know that someday I will die, and I have faith that I will survive the death of my body. And as I explained in an earlier chapter, I seem often to be overcome by moods and emotions that suggest that the ultimate satisfaction I seek is unattainable in this life.

One example of how the test of the inner world can be put to good use is Lewis's *Mere Christianity*.[6] He begins by getting his readers to reflect on their own moral consciousness. Each human being makes distinctions between right and wrong. Even people who profess to be ethical relativists act contrary to their profession when they themselves have been wronged. When someone wrongs us, our protests make it clear that we believe the other person is aware of the same moral law. The thing that interests Lewis about the remarks people make when they quarrel is this:

> . . . the man who makes them is not merely saying that the other man's behaviour does not happen to please him. He is appealing to some kind of standard of behaviour which he expects the other man to know about. And the other man very seldom replies: "To hell with your standard." Nearly always he tries to make out that what he has been doing does not really go against the standard, or that if it does there is some special excuse. He pretends there is some special reason in this particular case why the person who took the seat first should not keep it, or that things were quite different when he was given the bit of orange, or that something has turned up which lets him off

[6]Lewis, *Mere Christianity* (New York: Macmillan, 1960), especially book 1.

keeping his promise. It looks, in fact, very much as if both parties had in mind some kind of Law or Rule of fair play or decent behaviour or morality or whatever you like to call it, about which they really agreed. And they have. If they had not, they might, of course, fight like animals, but they could not *quarrel* in the human sense of the word. Quarrelling means trying to show that the other man is in the wrong. And there would be no sense in trying to do that unless you and he had some sort of agreement as to what Right and Wrong are; just as there would be no sense in saying that a footballer had committed a foul unless there was some agreement about the rules of football.[7]

What conditions best explain the fact of human moral consciousness? What worldview best accounts for this information about our inner world? Lewis goes on to test several competing worldviews in terms of their adequacy as an explanation for this phenomenon. He dismisses materialistic views of the universe because they cannot account for moral consciousness. He rejects pantheism because a pantheistic God is beyond good and evil; no real moral distinctions are possible in a pantheistic universe. He rejects dualism (the belief in two coequal and coeternal deities, one good and the other evil) because it cannot explain how we know which of the two "ultimate" principles is good.[8]

One reason why many tend to concentrate on the outer world as the major empirical test of worldviews may be the difficulties that accompany efforts to look "inward." Edward John Carnell argues:

> When formulating a philosophy of life, I contend that the least accessible fact, and thus the most baffling to isolate and classify, is the complex moral and spiritual environment of the philosopher himself. Most efforts at abstraction fail to impress the common man be-

[7]Ibid., 17–18.
[8]Ibid., book 2, chap. 1. Of course, there cannot be two ultimate principles. Such a claim contradicts the meaning of *ultimate*.

cause sages seldom take time to interpret life from within the center of their own perspective as individuals. . . . A world view remains truncated to the degree that a thinker fails to deal with data gained by a humble participation in the moral and spiritual environment. . . . What it means to be held in a moral and spiritual environment can only be learned as one acquaints himself with the realities that already hold him from existence itself. This pilgrimage into inwardness is a painfully personal responsibility, for only the individual himself has access to the secrets of his moral and spiritual life.[9]

But no matter how hard it may be to look honestly at our inner self, we are right in being suspicious of those whose defense of a worldview ignores or rejects the inner world.

THE TEST OF PRACTICE

Worldviews should be tested not only in the philosophy classroom but also in the laboratory of life. It is one thing for a worldview to pass certain theoretical tests (reason and experience); it is another for the worldview also to pass an important practical test, namely, can the person who professes that worldview live *consistently* in harmony with the system he professes? Or do we find that he is forced to live according to beliefs borrowed from a competing system? Such a discovery, I suggest, should produce more than embarrassment.

This practical test played an important role in the work of the Christian thinker Francis Schaeffer. Thomas Morris explains Schaeffer's position:

No non-Christian can be consistent in the correspondence of at least some of their daily thoughts and actions with the relevant conclusion which would

[9]Edward John Carnell, *The Case for Biblical Christianity*, ed. Ronald Nash (Grand Rapids: Eerdmans, 1969), 58.

logically follow from their basic sets of presuppositions. The orientation of [Schaeffer's] position was that
non-Christians would have a difficult time of consistently working out their presuppositions as they lived
in the context of their own [inner world] and the
external world.[10]

Schaeffer's practical or existential test helped lay the
foundation for Morris's punch line:

> Only the presuppositions of historic Christianity both
> adequately explain and correspond with the two envi-
> ronments in which every man must live: the external
> world with its form and complexity; and the internal
> world of the man's own characteristics as a human
> being. This "inner world" includes such human quali-
> ties "as a desire for significance, love, and meaning,
> and fear of nonbeing, among others."[11]

One thing should be clear: any reader who comes to
believe that Schaeffer's comments are true will have a
powerful reason to accept the Christian worldview. We
should keep his words in mind as we continue our journey.

A QUESTION ABOUT METHOD

In the first part of this chapter, I examined several
different tests that can be used to support judgments about
the adequacy of competing worldviews. I now want to carry
the matter of testing worldviews a bit further by throwing
light on the kind of method or procedure I am recommend-

[10]Thomas Morris, *Francis Schaeffer's Apologetics* (Grand Rapids:
Baker, 1987), 21–22. Schaeffer's work has been misunderstood, ironically
enough, by a number of evangelical thinkers. For one attempt to set the
record straight, see Ronald Nash, "The Life of the Mind and the Way of
Life," in *Francis Schaeffer: Portraits of the Man and His Work*, ed. Lane T.
Dennis (Westchester, Ill.: Crossway, 1986), chap. 3. Also worth consult-
ing, in the same book, is the chapter by Lane Dennis titled "Schaeffer and
His Critics."

[11]Ibid., 21. In this paragraph, Morris is both paraphrasing and
quoting Schaeffer.

ing. One thing in particular I want to make clear is that my method is *not* deductive.

History's most famous syllogism[12] begins with the major premise that "all men are mortal," provides a minor premise that is more specific ("Socrates is a man"), and ends with a conclusion ("Socrates is mortal"), the truth of which is already implicit in the premises. The validity of a deductive argument is a function of its form, not its content. That is, *any* argument is valid that has the same logical form[13] as this famous model regardless of the particular words that may be substituted. The conclusion of a valid deductive argument never contains information that is not already present in the premises. The major advantage of any valid deductive argument is that it provides *logical certainty*. In the case of any valid argument, if the premises are true, then the conclusion *must* be true.[14]

Inductive reasoning also assumes a number of different forms. It may involve reasoning from a few specific cases to a generalization about the many. Or it may involve what is called analogical reasoning: because two things are thought to be alike or analogous in one respect, one infers that they are alike in another respect. The key form in which inductive reasoning differs from deductive is the

[12]Deductive reasoning need not take the form of my famous example. Deductive reasoning may be hypothetical (If p, then q; p; therefore, q) or disjunctive in form (either p or q; not q; therefore, p). Obviously, this paragraph is not supposed to replace an entire textbook on logic.

[13]The logical form of our syllogism can be made clear by substituting letters for the terms of the original argument: All A is B; All C is A; therefore, all C is B. Any argument having this form is valid. Other valid and invalid forms of the categorical syllogism are identified in standard logic texts.

[14]Every beginning logic student also learns that validity and truth should be distinguished. Truth (or falsity) is a property of the particular propositions that make up an argument. Validity (or invalidity) is a property of arguments. If the premises of a valid argument are true, then the conclusion must be true. But if one or more of any argument's premises are false, nothing may be inferred about the truth or falsity of the conclusion.

absence of logical certainty in inductive thinking. The most that any inductive argument can provide is probability.

Since the method recommended in this chapter is not deductive, its conclusions lack logical certainty; probability in this kind of reasoning is unavoidable. Some people find this hard to understand and to accept. They act as though recommending a procedure that provides "only" probability is not simply suspicious; it is downright subversive. Since such judgments manifest a clear misunderstanding of what is or is not possible in inductive reasoning, I offer the following explanation.

Several types of reasoning illustrate the approach I have in mind. British philosopher Basil Mitchell has compared the testing of worldviews to the way in which one seeks the correct interpretation of a written text [15] Every student of the Bible and other great literature knows how difficult it can be sometimes to grasp the author's meaning in a particular phrase, sentence, or paragraph. The best interpretation is the one that most faithfully takes into account the message of the entire text within its historical and literary context. Before a final interpretation is suggested, one must study carefully the vocabulary, the textual context, and the historical setting in which the text was written. The most likely interpretation is the one that fits best all the relevant information. No matter how carefully the interpreter does her work, no interpretation can ever achieve logical certainty. Competing interpretations will be more or less probable, depending on how well they fit.

The interpretation of historical events is another example of the kind of reasoning used in evaluating worldviews. When Elizabeth I became queen of England in 1558, her official title read: "Elizabeth, by the Grace of God, Queen of England, France, and Spain, Defender of the Faith, etc."[16] This raises an interesting question. What is that

[15]See Basil Mitchell, *The Justification of Religious Belief* (New York: Seabury, 1973), 40ff.
[16]I have taken the liberty of changing spelling and punctuation to make the title easier to read.

"etc." doing in the queen's title? Here is something that seems to cry out for explanation. Ernest Nagel summarizes one historian's attempt to make sense of it.

> The legal historian F. W. Maitland proposed the following explanation. He first showed that the ["etc."] in the proclamation was not there by inadvertence but had been introduced deliberately. He also pointed out that Elizabeth was confronted with the alternatives either of acknowledging [with her half-sister, the late Queen Mary] the ecclesiastical supremacy of the Pope or of voiding the Marian statutes and breaking with Rome as her father had done—a decision for either alternative being fraught with grave perils, because the alignment of political and military forces both at home and abroad which favored each alternative was unsettled. Maitland therefore argued that in order to avoid committing herself to either alternative for the moment, Elizabeth employed an ambiguous formulation in the proclamation of her title—a formulation which could be made compatible with any decision she might eventually make. In consequence, according to his own succinct summary statement of the explanation, "So we might expand the symbol thus: ["etc."]—and (if the future events shall so decide, but no further or otherwise) of the Church of England and also of Ireland upon earth the Supreme Head."[17]

The historian approaches his material much as the interpreter approaches his text. Both are confronted with the challenge to understand and to explain something. Both gather as much relevant information as they can. Both advance a theory or hypothesis; perhaps other interpreters and historians offer competing hypotheses. Maitland's hypothesis was that the appearance of the "etc." in Queen Elizabeth's title was not an accident on someone's part; it was there for a reason. And the reason is to be found in the

[17]Ernest Nagel, *The Structure of Science* (New York: Harcourt, Brace & World, 1961), 552. Nagel's quote come from F. W. Maitland's "Elizabethan Gleanings," in Maitland's *Collected Papers* (London, 1911), 3:157–65.

perilous historical circumstances that obtained when Elizabeth ascended to the throne. To have laid claim explicitly to headship of the Church of England in 1558 would certainly have led to war with Spain and possible insurrection within England. To renounce any further claim to such authority over the English church at that time seemed unwise. And so, Maitland theorized, Elizabeth decided to stall for time by including that apparently innocuous "etc." in her official title. Later, when future events made her options clearer and a final decision safer, she could announce all that the "etc." included. Is Maitland's interpretation correct? Any final decision depends on whether it fits all that we know about the times and about the makeup of Elizabeth's mind better than any rival interpretation. Once again, the most that any interpretation can hope to achieve is a high degree of probability.

A third analogy is found in the processes by which fictional detectives like Sherlock Holmes and Hercule Poirot go about solving mysteries. Most people who read the novels of Sir Arthur Conan Doyle and Agatha Christie attempt to "solve" the mystery before the correct answer is finally revealed. Consciously or unconsciously, the reader advances and withdraws various hypotheses (proposed solutions) as the plot unwinds. The disclosure of new information may disconfirm one theory and give greater plausibility to another. The correct answer is the one that best fits all the clues.

Thus far, one property, *coherence*, characterizes the best textual interpretations, historical explanations, and solutions to mystery novels. The superior theory is the one that coheres best with everything else we know; the better interpretation, explanation, or answer is the one that most nearly fits all the data.

Another example of the procedure for evaluating worldviews that I recommend can be found in the way scientists seek an explanation for a phenomenon. They ask, "What conditions make sense of this situation?" They usually find it necessary to consider a number of possibilities. The various alternatives they examine become hypotheses, which are then confirmed or disconfirmed by how well they explain the phenomenon. Which explanation, which hypothesis, best makes sense of this situation? This is similar to the way a literary scholar settles on the meaning of a text, to the way a historian reaches a decision about the explanation of a historical event, and to the way Sherlock Holmes solved a crime. The procedure is similar to the way we evaluate worldviews. Honest inquirers say to themselves, "Here is what I know about the inner and outer worlds. Now which touchstone proposition, which worldview, does the best job of making sense of all this?"

Literary scholars, historians, detectives, scientists, and worldview examiners who are good at their job don't stop with the first piece of information that confirms their theory; they keep looking. As the amount of confirmatory information increases, so too does the probability of the truth of the hypothesis increase. A large number of observations taken together provides a cumulative case enhancing the likelihood that the hypothesis is true. Thomas Morris provides a helpful illustration:

> Suppose we are in a windowless room and we are considering two rival hypotheses: It is raining outside and it is sunny outside. There are many events that would be expected to occur if the rain hypothesis were true, but not if the sun hypothesis were true, such as: water beating on the roof, a friend coming in soaked, water running in the street, etc. Suppose we hear the sound of water beating on the roof (an observation of one of the above events). This observation confirms and raises the probability of the rain hypothesis. Do we then *know* that the rain hypothesis is true, that it is raining outside?[18]

The answer, of course, is no. Even though we happen to hear water beating on the roof, it might be due to

[18]Morris, *Schaeffer's Apologetics*, 96.

someone's spraying water there and possibly the sun is shining outside. Morris continues:

> Likewise, suppose that we see a friend enter the room soaking wet. This observation also confirms and raises the probability of the rain hypothesis, but neither does it prove conclusively that it is true. The man with the water hose could have drenched him. Finally, suppose that we hear the sound of passing cars on wet pavement. This would also be a confirming observation, but again not alone decisive, since it may be that the city street sweeper has just washed the street, and the weather itself is beautifully sunny. Although no one of the above observations would conclusively prove that it is raining outside, their cumulative effect would raise the probability of the rain hypothesis so high that we would be fully justified in believing that it is raining outside. This belief can be said to be a justified subjective response to and result of the cumulative probability given to the rain hypothesis by the three confirming observations.[19]

Morris is quick to admit that in our daily lives, we do not operate in terms of such a formal procedure. We do not consciously advance and then sort through competing hypotheses simply to reach a decision about whether the sun is shining outside. But he concludes that if one hypothesis or explanation fits better with our observations of the inner and outer worlds, if one hypothesis make better sense theoretically and existentially, would we not be foolish to reject it in favor of a hypothesis that fared less well?[20]

[19]Ibid., 96–97.
[20]I don't want to press the analogy of a scientific hypothesis too far. For one thing, it would be a serious error to regard a faith commitment to Jesus Christ as analogous to the way we sometimes put forward tentative hypotheses. But at the same time, faith in Jesus Christ and our belief in the truth of the Christian worldview *are* related to information and experiences that serve to confirm or disconfirm such belief. Jesus did not ask his followers to believe against all reason or in the absence of reason. On the contrary, he gave them reasons *to* believe. I discuss some aspects of the

THE PROBLEM OF CERTAINTY

But what about certainty? Individuals might ask, is there not something sacrilegious about a purported justification of religious belief that leaves us with nothing more than probability? Is there not an alternative approach that would allow us to believe with certainty? And if so, would not such an alternative have more to commend it than, say, a system that promises nothing more than probability?

Questions like these reveal a serious misunderstanding on the part of the questioners. They need instruction in the difference between the kind of certainty found in mathematics and logic (call it logical certainty) and that available in other areas (call it psychological or moral certainty).

Logical certainty is found exclusively in such areas as formal logic, geometry, and mathematics. Examples of propositions that can be known with logical certainty include these:

1. Seven plus five equals twelve.
2. No object can be round and square at the same time in the same sense.
3. Either Richard Nixon was the thirty-sixth president of the United States or he was not the thirty-sixth president of the United States.

Logical certainty is limited to this kind of thinking. Number one is true, of course, because of the laws of mathematics. Number two is true because of the law of noncontradiction. Number three is true because of the law of the excluded middle. In order for any proposition to be certain in this logical sense, it must be necessarily true or false.

But propositions such as "Jesus Christ rose bodily from the grave," "God created the world," and "the Bible contains sixty-six books" cannot attain logical certainty;

relationship between faith and reason in my book *Christian Faith and Historical Understanding*, chap. 8.

nor can informative propositions about history, geography, physics, astronomy, or home economics; nor can *any* worldview. Once one leaves the arena of purely formal reasoning for the world of blood, sweat, and tears, one is required to abandon logical certainty for probability. Informative judgments about particular things and events (or collections of things and events) can never rise above probability. But this is hardly cause for regret. As Edward John Carnell once observed:

> This admission that Christianity's proof for the resurrection of Christ cannot rise above probability is not a form of weakness; it is rather an indication that the Christian is in possession of a worldview which is making a sincere effort to come to grips with actual history. Christianity is not a deductively necessary system of thought which has been spun out of a philosopher's head, wholly indifferent to the march of human history below it.[21]

But even though no worldview can rise above logical probability, it may still be believed with moral certainty. A single proposition or system of propositions that is only probable in the logical sense may still generate certainty in the psychological or moral sense. Carnell adds:

> Rational probability and complete or perfect moral assurance are by no means incompatible. We are morally assured that there was a man named George Washington, though the rational evidence for his existence is only probable. All the mind need be convinced of is coherence to be morally assured . . . The arguments for Christianity— though but probable in rational strength—move the Christian to act upon the supposition of the truth of the Christian faith.[22]

Before acting—often in matters that could have a significant impact on our lives and happiness—we seldom

[21]Edward John Carnell, *An Introduction to Christian Apologetics* (Grand Rapids: Eerdmans, 1948), 114–15.
[22]Ibid., 118.

stop and engage in a process of making formal inferences. Before entering an elevator, for example, few normal people enter information about the elevator into a portable computer to check the probabilities of reaching their destination safely. We often act in life with far greater assurance (moral certainty) than the evidence warrants. We do not really *know* many of the things that for practical purposes we assume. We act on probabilities so strong that for practical purposes they become indistinguishable from certainties.

To demand logical certainty in the matters under consideration in this book is bizarre. My admission that we must deal in terms of probabilities (in the logical sense) is not a defect; it is a clue that we are dealing responsibly with an inescapable feature of the real world.□

Chapter 4

A Further Look at the Test of Reason

During my visit to the Soviet Union, which I mentioned earlier, I presented a lecture on worldview thinking in general and upon the superiority of the Christian worldview in particular to an audience of university graduates. After the presentation, an obviously upset young lady asked that we debate some of the points I had made. Later, when I met with her and a translator, she introduced herself as a philosophy instructor. While she was complimentary about many facets of my discussion, one thing troubled her greatly; that was the importance I had given to the laws of logic, an importance that surprised her.

I will let you in on a little secret. Whenever anyone accuses me of being a rationalist,[1] of placing too much emphasis upon the laws of logic, I regard this as a compliment—no matter how the statement is meant by my critic. In the case of my Russian critic, it took me several minutes to determine precisely where she was coming from. At first I thought she was a traditional, hard-

---

[1]The word *rationalist* has many meanings. In this context, I am a rationalist in the sense that I believe (a) that human beings can know things not derivable through sense experience; and (b) that the laws of logic apply to every level of being. Whenever we encounter a logical contradiction, we can be certain that we are in the presence of error.

core Marxist-Leninist who was objecting to my emphasis upon the law of noncontradiction because it conflicted with the Marxist concept of the dialectic.[2] In fact, it wasn't until a second meeting the next day that I realized she was a convert to a strange Russian version of what we in the United States call New Age thinking. She was a proponent of a kind of pantheistic mysticism in which "ultimate truth" transcends all the usual canons of reason and logic. Once that became clear, I offered her some of the arguments that will appear later in this chapter. While the Russian philosopher left our last meeting unpersuaded, we parted as friends, and I have a standing invitation to address her students the next time I visit Moscow.

I mention this because even though most people who reject Christianity treat it as a refuge for enemies of reason, the truth is that there may be no worldview in the history of the human race that has a higher regard for the laws of logic. Having made this claim, however, I must now add an important qualification. This respect for the laws of logic is an essential part of the Christian worldview when that worldview is understood correctly. Regrettably, there are large numbers of Christians who are irrationalists in their understanding and portrayal of the Christian faith. But, I contend, such people are deficient in their grasp of the Christian worldview and in their understanding of what the laws of logic—especially the law of noncontradiction—are all about.

IS RELIGION AGAINST LOGIC?

In a 1955 article titled "Mysticism and Human Reason," former Princeton University philosopher W. T. Stace wrote, "God is utterly and forever beyond the reach of the logical intellect or of any intellectual comprehension,

---

[2]We have no good reason to detour here into the mysteries of the Marxist dialectic. Suffice it to say that for the few adherents of this bizarre theory who are still alive, neither truth nor reason is stable or fixed but is constantly changing.

and that in consequence when we try to comprehend his nature intellectually, contradictions appear in our thinking."[3] As Stace saw things, "any attempt to reach God through logic, through the conceptual, logical intellect, is doomed."[4] Then in no time at all Stace moves to the more extreme position that religious believers should completely reject logic when dealing with God.

Stace, himself a mystic, ridicules other mystics for yielding to their rational impulses and seeking ways to eliminate contradictions in their thinking about God. The proper course, for Stace, is to glory in the contradictions. As Stace puts it,

> My own belief is that all attempts to rationalize the paradox, to make it logically acceptable, are futile because the paradoxes of religion and of mysticism are irresoluble by the human intellect. My view is that they never have been, they never can be, and they never will be resolved, or made logical. . . . When you say that God is incomprehensible, one thing you mean is just that these contradictions break out in our intellect and cannot be resolved, no matter how clever or how good a logician you may be.[5]

Stace is especially critical of Buddhist mystics who attempt to remove contradictions in their system by postulating two Brahmans, a higher and lower. "One may be quite sure," Stace advises, "that this is the wrong solution because the religious intuition is preemptory that God is one and not two."[6] Logic then simply does not apply in religion. Stace is not simply saying that religion could be unreasonable in the sense that it discusses things that are above human reason. For Stace, religion is actually against logic. "Should we say that there is contradiction in the nature of God himself, in the ultimate being? Well, if we

[3]W. T. Stace, "Mysticism and Human Reason," *University of Arizona Bulletin Series* 26 (1955), 19.
[4]Ibid., 20.
[5]Ibid., 17.
[6]Ibid.

were to say that, I think that we shouldn't be saying anything very unusual or very shocking."[7]

At first Stace sounds like one who thinks that God is above the laws of reason. But let us observe the problems that Stace's irrationalism creates for him. If Stace was correct and logic has no relevance to the kind of mysticism he represented, it is difficult to understand most of what he wrote. For example, why, given his repudiation of logic, did he criticize Buddhists who rejected the unity of God in favor of two Brahmans? After all, once logic is disavowed, God can be both one *and* two (or two thousand) at the same time and in the same sense. If a distinction can be drawn between a monistic God and a dualistic or pluralistic deity, than logic must have some relevance after all. Once logic is denied, inconsistency becomes a virtue.

IS RELIGION ABOVE LOGIC?

Thomas Torrance, a leading theologian in the Church of Scotland and a disciple of Karl Barth, is one of a number of Protestant thinkers who seems to insist on a distinction between God's logic and a different, lower human logic. Indeed, Torrance seems to believe that because the forms of "human logic" cannot be extended to the transcendent God of the Christian faith, human logic, human reasoning, and human concepts are all inadequate for a knowledge of the Christian God.[8] He writes that human "ideas and conceptions and analogies and words are too limited and narrow and poor for knowledge of God."[9] A careful reading of Torrance suggests that he thinks human knowledge about God is impossible and human forms of reasoning are completely incapable of understanding truth and reason as it exists in the mind of God.

But several problems with Torrance's religious irra-

[7]Ibid., 18–19.
[8]See Thomas F. Torrance, *Theological Science* (London: Oxford Univ. Press, 1969), 54, 153, 205, and other passages.
[9]Ibid., 49.

tionalism become immediately obvious. For one thing, if the principles of logic are as tentative and mutable as Torrance suggests, how can one have any confidence in the validity of Torrance's own reasoning? After all, if God himself cannot reveal timeless truths or universally valid information to us, what leads Torrance to think that he can? His book purports to be true and to contain universally valid information. Does Torrance then believe that he can do something that God cannot?

Dr. Carl F. H. Henry notes, in utter amazement, that in all of his contentions

> Torrance seems to be privy to objective propositional knowledge about God which his methodology pointedly disallows to other human beings. From what source, for example, did Torrance derive the information that there is an ultimate objectivity which cannot be enclosed within the creaturely objectivities through which we encounter it, an objectivity that indefinitely transcends creaturely objectivities.[10]

Torrance's repeated use of assumptions he denies to others does not speak well of his consistency. As Henry goes on to point out, Torrance's position reduces to skepticism:

> The insistence of a logical gulf between human conceptions and God as the object of religious knowledge is erosive of knowledge and cannot escape a reduction to skepticism. Concepts that by definition are inadequate to the truth of God cannot be made to compensate for logical deficiency by appealing either to God's omnipotence or to his grace. Nor will it do to call for restructuring of logic in the interest of knowledge of God. Whoever calls for higher logic must preserve the existing laws of logic to escape pleading the cause of illogical nonsense.[11]

[10]Carl F. H. Henry, *God, Revelation and Authority* (Waco, Tex.: Word, 1979), 3:223.
[11]Ibid., 3:229.

If God really does have a logic all his own, then no criteria can exist that can possibly aid humans to distinguish between Yahweh and Satan. "If the law of contradiction is irrelevant in the sphere of transcendent ontology, then God and the not-God, the divine and the demonic, cannot be assuredly differentiated."[12]

A disavowal of logic in a way similar to what we find in Thomas Torrance appears in the philosophy of Herman Dooyeweerd, a Dutch thinker whose work is central to the thought of some Calvinist thinkers in Grand Rapids, Michigan, and at the small Institute for Christian Studies in Toronto, Ontario.

It is not necessary to go into the details of Dooyeweerd's philosophy.[13] What is important for our present purposes is Dooyeweerd's theory of "the Boundary." The doctrine of the Boundary is the most important way followers of Dooyeweerd emphasize the sovereignty and transcendence of God. All of God's creation, they say, is subject to various laws such as the laws of physics, the laws of biology, the laws of mathematics, the laws of thinking, the laws of economics, and so on. Because God is the Lawgiver, he himself is not subject to the laws that govern his creation. Law then constitutes a boundary between God and the creation. The laws that apply *under* the Boundary do not apply to God who is above all law.

Dooyeweerd's teaching seems innocuous enough until one realizes how the followers of Dooyeweerd apply the theory to human reason. In their hands, what could have been a helpful metaphor is interpreted in a way that entails a total and complete break between God's logic and human logic. For the followers of Dooyeweerd, the laws of logic, of valid inference, exist *only* on the human side of the Boundary. The result of this is the establishment of a gap or wall that Dooyeweerdians think exists between the mind of God and the human mind. In the words of L. Kalsbeek,

[12]Ibid., 2:60.
[13]I did this myself to some extent in my *Dooyeweerd and the Amsterdam Philosophy*.

humans "can only think meaningfully about what lies on
our side of that boundary. Due to the limitations of our
creaturely thinking as a result of its subjection to the law
[in this case the law of logic], we can only engage in
meaningless speculation when it comes to questions and
pronouncements about whatever lies on the other side of
the boundary."[14]

The implication is clear. Those who hold such a view
believe it is impossible for any human being to think
meaningfully about God. Rationality exists totally below
the Boundary. Logic, the principles of valid inference,
cannot apply beyond the Boundary, from which it follows
that there is no continuity between the Creator and the
creature. Such a view seems a clear denial of the image of
God in humans. But this problem aside, the position is also
self-contradictory.

After all, since human thought and human concepts
can never reach the truth about God, where do the
Dooyeweerdians get their abundant knowledge about God?
As we have seen, Dooyeweerdians believe that human
reasoning can be "valid" only on the human side of the
Boundary. No human reasoning can bring us to a knowledge
of what is true beyond the Boundary. If human reason is
valid only on this side of the Boundary, then any inferences
the Christian might draw from the Bible (such as the belief
that God is transcendent) must be an illegitimate application of human reason. While Alvin Plantinga wrote the
following words in reference to a different type of religious
agnosticism, his comments apply with equal force to the
irrational and skeptical implications of all who would
attempt to distinguish between God's logic and human
logic. This kind of thinking, Plantinga wrote,

> begins in a pious and commendable concern for God's
> greatness and majesty and augustness; but it ends in
> agnosticism and in incoherence. For if none of our

[14]L. Kalsbeek, *Contours of a Christian Philosophy* (Toronto: Wedge,
1975), 74–75.

concepts apply to God [or if none of our inferences extend to God], then there is nothing we can know or truly believe of him—not even what is affirmed in the creeds or revealed in the Scriptures. And if there is nothing we can know or truly believe of him, then, of course, we cannot know or truly believe that none of our concepts apply to him. The view . . . is fatally ensnarled in self-referential absurdity.[15]

When Christian irrationalists claim that no proposition can mean the same thing to God and to humans, that our knowledge and God's knowledge do not coincide at a single point, and that God's logic and man's logic are totally different, it is time to object. Notice how each of these claims assumes knowledge about God, knowledge that says something about what lies beyond the Boundary. While the assorted rejections of logic found in the writings of Thomas Torrance and the followers of Herman Dooyeweerd are pious nonsense, they are still nonsense.

ANOTHER LOOK AT THE LAW OF NONCONTRADICTION

Earlier, I defined the law of noncontradiction as the claim that "*A* cannot be both *B* and non-*B* at the same time in the same sense." There is a helpful way of seeing the essential point to this claim. Consider the following box in which I have located the terms *B* and non-*B*.

Let us suppose that the larger box represents the entire universe in the sense that if anything (call it *A*) exists, it exists inside the box. It might also be helpful if the reader refrains from confusing this box with the quite different box that refers to nature, which I discuss elsewhere in the book. I am talking about something else here, so forget that other box. Now our larger box contains a smaller box that I have called *B*. This box represents a class or group or set of things

---

[15]Alvin Plantinga, *Does God Have a Nature?* (Milwaukee: Marquette Univ. Press, 1980), 26.

that have something essential in common. Hence, *B* could represent the class of all dogs or all stars or all humans. Remember that *B* is not all of those different things together. It is only one of them, any one of them.

Non-*B* is what we call the complementary class of *B*. This simply means that if, for example, the box we have called *B* represents the class of all dogs, then non-*B* stands for everything else in the universe that is *not* a dog. The complementary class of non-*B* includes cats, fish, George Bush and Saddam Hussein, the Ohio River, Mount Everest, the moon—in short, anything in the universe that is something other than a dog. If *B* represented the class of all human beings, then non-*B* would include everything in the universe that is not a human.

Now, all that the law of noncontradiction says is this: if something, if anything (call it *A*) is a member of the class we have called *B*, then A *cannot* under any condition *also* (at the same time and in the same sense) be a member of the complementary class of non *B*.

Consider an example that makes obvious the meaning of all this: It is impossible for Socrates to be both man and non-man. Since the class of non-man is the complement of the class of man, the claim that Socrates is also a member of the class of non-*B* (non-man) is tantamount to saying that Socrates is everything else in the universe except man. Thus, anyone who claims that Socrates can be both man and non-man is really saying that Socrates can be a dog, star, tree, and indeed everything else in the universe at the same time. Gordon H. Clark outlines the implications:

> If contradictory statements are true of the same subject at the same time, evidently all things will be the same thing. Socrates will be a ship, a house, as well as a man. But if precisely the same attributes attach to Crito that attach to Socrates it follows that Socrates is Crito. Not only so, but the ship in the harbor, since it has the same list of attributes too, will be identified with this Socrates-Crito person. In fact, everything will be everything. Therefore everything will be the same thing. All differences among things will vanish and all will be one.[16]

Such is the nonsense that follows from any denial of the law of noncontradiction.

PROVING THE LAW OF NONCONTRADICTION

Strictly speaking, the law of noncontradiction cannot be proved. The reason is simple. Any argument offered as proof for the law of noncontradiction would of necessity have to assume the law as part of the proof. Hence, any direct proof of the law would end up being circular. It would beg the question.

But while no direct demonstration of the principle of noncontradiction exists, there is a persuasive indirect argument that assumes two forms. In its first form, the indirect proof is built upon the claim that significant human action requires us to presuppose the law of noncontradiction. If there is no real difference between B and its complement non-B, then there is no difference between driving north on the interstate highway and driving south. Even worse, there is no difference between driving on the right side of a divided highway and driving on the left side. But, of course, there *is* a difference.

[16]Gordon H. Clark, *Thales to Dewey* (Grand Rapids: Baker, 1981), 103.

I once heard of a college graduate who was called into his local office of the Internal Revenue Service for an audit. One reason for his trouble was his failure over several years to file a tax return. When asked by the IRS agent why he had failed to file, the youth replied that while in college he had learned that the law of noncontradiction is an optional, non-necessary principle. Once he had learned that there is no difference between *B* and non-*B*, it was only a matter of time before he realized that no difference exists between filing a tax return and not filing a tax return. "That's very interesting," said the tax agent. "I've never heard that one before. Since you believe that no difference exists between *B* and non-*B*, I'm sure you also believe that there is no difference between being in jail and not being in jail!"

In an earlier chapter, I pointed out that any proposition that entails a false or absurd proposition must be rejected. In other words, if *p* implies *q* and *q* is false (or absurd), *p* must be false (or absurd). The denial of the law of noncontradiction necessarily implies all kinds of absurd consequences, one of which is the impossibility of significant human action. This unacceptable consequence reflects badly on the original premise that led to it.

But another unacceptable consequence follows from any denial of our principle. For anyone foolish enough to doubt or deny the law of noncontradiction, significant speech also becomes impossible. If the critic of the law says anything significant, then he must make use of the very law he is attempting to refute. And, of course, if he says nothing, then we need not worry about his opinions since he refuses to make them known.

This second argument contains two elements: (1) On the level of language, if one is to speak significantly, contrary meanings may not be attributed to the same word at the same time and in the same sense; and (2) on the level of being, as opposed to the level of language, contrary properties may not belong to the same subject at the same time and in the same sense.

This position is clearly at odds with the position, so

popular in much recent philosophy, that regards the law of noncontradiction as a purely formal law or as an arbitrary stipulation useful for constructing symbolic systems. The law of noncontradiction is not simply a law of thought. It is a law of thought because it is first a law of being. Nor is the law something someone can take or leave. The denial of the law of noncontradiction leads to absurdity. It is impossible meaningfully to deny the laws of logic. If the law of noncontradiction is denied, then nothing has meaning. If the laws of logic do not first mean what they say, nothing else can have meaning, including the denial of the laws.[17]

THE NOTION OF SELF-REFERENTIAL ABSURDITY

An important application of the principle of noncontradiction is the discovery of positions that suffer from the dreaded disease of self-referential absurdity. This condition exists whenever the application of a theory to itself involves one in a necessary falsehood or logical nonsense. We encountered this notion in an earlier chapter when we saw how skepticism turns out to be a self-defeating position. Whenever we find someone saying that no one can know anything, it is only natural to wonder whether the skeptic knows *that*.

Strangers to philosophy are often surprised to discover how many self-referentially absurd positions one can find in the history of philosophy. One example of such a system is the Logical Positivism that was so popular in Western Europe, Great Britain, and the United States during the 1930s and 1940s.[18]

The touchstone proposition of Logical Positivism was something called the verification principle. Logical positiv-

---

[17]Students of the history of philosophy will know how indebted the argument of the last few pages is to Aristotle. For more on this subject, see my *The Word of God and the Mind of Man*, chap. 10.

[18]The book that came to be regarded as the most influential statement of Logical Positivism was A. J. Ayer's *Language, Truth and Logic* (London: Gollancz, 1936).

ists thought they had discovered a criterion of meaningfulness that would exclude all kinds of claims they found distasteful, for example, statements like "God exists." Only two kinds of propositions can have meaning, the positivists argued: those that are true because of the meaning of their constituent terms (called analytic statements)[19] and those that are verifiable by sense experience (called synthetic statements). Positivists delighted in showing, or so they thought, that theological, metaphysical, and ethical statements failed to meet either criterion of meaningfulness. And so because such statements were neither analytic (true or false by virtue of the meanings of their words) nor synthetic (true or false because they were verifiable by experience) they were discarded as meaningless. This meant that statements like "God exists" were neither true nor false; they were meaningless!

The positivists used their verification principle like a sledgehammer, smashing a great many of the traditional positions in philosophy, including beliefs about God, the soul, and morality. At least they did so until people began to ask about the cognitive status of the positivists' hallowed principle. What kind of statement is *it*? As things turned out, the positivists' criterion of meaning showed itself to be meaningless because it could be classified as neither an analytic nor a synthetic statement. Efforts to rescue the verification principle failed.[20] So today it is difficult to find any philosopher who is willing to admit adherence to Logical Positivism. The movement is dead and quite properly so.

[19]Examples of analytic statements include tautologies like "Some spinsters are unmarried ladies" (which are necessarily true) and contradictions like "Some spinsters are married ladies" (which are necessarily false). An example of a synthetic statement would be "Some spinsters drive American-made cars."

[20]One could spend years reading nothing but criticisms of Logical Positivism. Two critiques of the verification principle from different perspectives are Alvin Plantinga, *God and Other Minds* (Ithaca: Cornell Univ. Press, 1967) and Brand Blanshard, *Reason and Analysis* (La Salle, Ill.: Open Court, 1962).

Many philosophers have argued that determinism, an essential element of the naturalistic worldview, is self-refuting. According to J. R. Lucas, if what the determinist says is true,

> he says it merely as the result of his heredity and environment, and of nothing else. He does not hold his determinist views because they are true, but because he has such-and-such stimuli; that is, not because the *structure* of the universe is such-and-such but only because the configuration of only part of the universe, together with the structure of the determinist's brain, is such as to produce that result. . . . Determinism, therefore, cannot be true, because if it was, we should not take the determinists' arguments as being really arguments, but as being only conditioned reflexes. Their statements should not be regarded as really claiming to be true, but only as seeking to cause us to respond in some way desired by them.[21]

H. P. Owen agrees that

> determinism is self-stultifying. If my mental processes are totally determined, I am totally determined either to accept or to reject determinism. But if the sole reason for my believing or not believing X is that I am causally determined to believe it I have no ground for holding that my judgment is true or false.[22]

Philosopher J. P Moreland is one of many who claim that physicalism, another corollary of naturalism, is also self-refuting. Physicalism is the position that "the only thing which exists is matter (where matter is defined by an

[21]J. R. Lucas, *Freedom of the Will* (Oxford: Clarendon Press, 1970), 114–15.

[22]H. P. Owen, *Christian Theism* (Edinburgh: T and T Clark, 1984), 118. It would be a mistake to confuse the total, mechanistic determinism being criticized here with the Reformed or Calvinistic worldview held by many Christians. It might be a helpful exercise for many to contemplate the important differences between Calvinism and the godless, mechanical determinism of a naturalistic worldview. Hint: Reformed Christians believe that God himself is independent of any determining processes in creation.

ideal, completed form of physics)."[23] According to a physicalist view of man, Moreland observes, "a human being is just a physical system. There is no mind or soul, just a brain and central nervous system."[24] Now, Moreland continues, "if one claims to know that physicalism is true, or to embrace it for good reasons, if one claims that [physicalism] is a rational position, which should be chosen on the basis of evidence, then this claim is self-refuting."[25] Moreland's reason for his position is that physicalism implies that rationality is impossible. Moreland's summary of his argument is impressive for both its brevity and its power:

> In sum, it is self-refuting to *argue* that one *ought* to *choose* physicalism *because* he should *see* that the *evidence* is *good* for physicalism. Physicalism cannot be offered as a rational theory because physicalism does away with the necessary preconditions for there to be such a thing as rationality. Physicalism usually denies intentionality [the capacity to have thoughts *about* other things] by reducing it to a physical relation of input/output, thereby denying that the mind is genuinely capable of having thoughts *about* the world. Physicalism denies the existence of propositions and nonphysical laws of logic and evidence which can be in minds and influence thinking. Physicalism denies the existence of a faculty capable of rational insight into these nonphysical laws and propositions, and it denies the existence of an enduring "I" which is present through the process of reflection. Finally, it denies the existence of a genuine agent who deliberates and chooses positions because they are rational, an act possible only if physical factors are not sufficient for determining future behavior [26]

[23] J. P. Moreland, *Scaling the Secular City* (Grand Rapids: Baker, 1987), 78.
[24] Ibid.
[25] Ibid., 92.
[26] Ibid., 96. Moreland astutely notes that his argument against physicalism does not commit what is sometimes called the genetic fallacy. According to this fallacy, it is a mistake to infer the falseness of a belief because of problems connected with the origin of the belief. Moreland's

As we have noted, some philosophical positions or systems seem to self-destruct in the sense that they are internally self-defeating. The charge has been leveled against at least two major tenets of the naturalistic worldview, namely, determinism and physicalism. Clearly, the charge of inconsistency should be taken seriously, so seriously in fact that in the next chapter I will examine two alleged inconsistencies within Christian theism. Before taking up those problems, however, I want to take a look at one more philosophical theory that suffers from the problem of self-referential absurdity.

EVIDENTIALISM

Many people who reject Christianity do so because they think it fails to offer enough evidence to make it a rational alternative in the arena of ideas. When Bertrand Russell, the famous British atheist, was asked how he would reply when God questions why he didn't believe (assuming of course that Russell would some day stand before God), Russell replied that he would tell God, "Not enough evidence, God. Not enough evidence."

The position that will be examined in this section lies at the foundation of Russell's answer. Indeed, it functions as an assumption in the thinking of most unbelievers. The name for this theory is *evidentialism*.

A nineteenth-century thinker named W. K. Clifford captured the essence of evidentialism in one sentence: "It is wrong always, everywhere, and for anyone, to believe anything upon insufficient evidence."[27] As Clifford saw it,

argument against physicalism, as he explains, "is not an example of genetic fallacy, for in order for there to even be such a fallacy, one must be able to distinguish the process of the origin of a belief. But if *all* the factors which cause our beliefs are physical, then such a distinction is itself impossible, for there would be no rational factors or rational agents which could be affected by them" (Ibid., 229).

[27]W. K. Clifford, "The Ethics of Belief," in *Readings in the Philosophy of Religion*, ed. Baruch A. Brody (Englewood Cliffs, N. J.: Prentice-Hall, 1974), 246. Clifford's essay was published in his *Lectures*

people have duties and responsibilities with respect to their acts of believing. This is especially so, Clifford thought, in the case of religious beliefs. According to him, there is never sufficient evidence or proof to support religious belief. Consequently, anyone who accepts a religious belief (such as the belief that God exists) is guilty of acting immorally, irresponsibly, and irrationally.

The argument of the typical anti-theistic evidentialist looks something like this:

1. It is irrational to accept theistic belief in the absence of sufficient evidence.
2. There is insufficient evidence to support belief in God.
3. Therefore, belief in God is irrational.[28]

Evidentialism often seems to hold that all beliefs are guilty until proved innocent. In actual practice, especially in Clifford's work and that of countless atheists who follow in his train, the claim usually assumes the form that all *religious* beliefs are guilty until proved innocent. While nonbelievers are never obligated to begin by proving that God does not exist, believers are supposedly under the obligation to prove that God does exist. This is an interesting example of academic imperialism.

THE REJECTION OF EVIDENTIALISM

As we have seen, many contemporary anti-theistic evidentialists believe the burden of proof always rests on the theist; religious beliefs should be presumed guilty until

and Essays (London: Macmillan, 1879) and has been reprinted in countless anthologies.

[28]For the record, I ought to mention that there are also religious evidentialists, those who accept the evidentialist thesis (proposition 1 of the above argument) but who believe there is sufficient evidence to support belief in God, who offer examples of that evidence (sometimes in the form of arguments for the existence of God) and who then conclude that belief in God is rational. For more on this, see my *Faith and Reason* (Grand Rapids: Zondervan, 1988), chaps. 5–8.

shown to be otherwise. It is always the believer's responsibility to produce reasons or evidence to support his belief, and if he fails, the proper conclusion is that the belief is irrational. Without supporting evidence, the believer's persistence in believing is an irrational and morally defective act.

During the decade of the 1980s, Notre Dame philosopher Alvin Plantinga challenged the evidentialist thesis and the casual rejection of Christian belief that usually accompanies it. Plantinga asks, "Why should we think a theist must have evidence, or reason to think there *is* evidence, if he is not to be irrational? Why not suppose, instead, that he is entirely within his epistemic rights[29] in believing in God's existence even if he has no argument or evidence at all?"[30] For the record, it should be noted that Plantinga thinks there may well be reasons that support belief in God. But even though such reasons may exist, those reasons (or that evidence) are not necessary to make such a belief rational. In other words, Plantinga challenges the first premise of the evidentialist's argument, noted earlier. The rationality of religious belief does not depend on the discovery of supporting arguments or evidence.

Plantinga has developed two arguments against Clifford's misguided thesis that "it is wrong always, everywhere, and for anyone, to believe anything on insufficient evidence" (taking the word *evidence* to mean argument or proof).

First, Clifford's view would, if accepted, undercut all epistemic activity. We believe countless things (and believe properly and rationally) without proof or evidence. We believe in the existence of other minds; we believe that the world continues to exist even when we are not perceiving

[29]A word of explanation about the phrase "epistemic rights": The word *epistemic* is derived from "epistemology," the noun often used to refer to the philosophical study of knowledge. Hence, "epistemic rights" are rights humans have with regard to such things as acts of believing.

[30]Alvin Plantinga, "Reason and Belief in God," in *Faith and Rationality*, ed. A. Plantinga and N. Wolterstorff (Notre Dame, Ind: Univ. of Notre Dame Press, 1983), 30.

it. There are countless things that we not only believe but have a *right* to believe even though we lack proof or evidence. If we followed Clifford and eliminated all beliefs for which no proof or evidence is supplied, we would lose our right to affirm a large number of important claims that only a fool would question. And so it is clear that we have a right to believe *some* things without evidence or proof. Since belief in God turns out to belong to the same family of beliefs as, for example, our belief in other minds or our belief in the continuing existence of the unperceived world, we also have a right to believe in God without supporting evidence or arguments.

Second, Clifford's thesis is self-defeating. For him, it is immoral to believe *anything* without proof. But where is the proof for his evidentialist claim? What evidence does he provide for his belief that it is immoral to believe anything in the absence of evidence? The fact is that he provides no evidence; nor could he.

Clifford began by warning his reader against acting immorally with respect to his epistemic activities. Then he turned around and acted "immorally" by advancing a thesis for which he provided no proof or evidence. He is confronted by a dilemma of his own making. Either evidentialism is false, or it fails the evidentialist's own test of rationality. If it is false, then believing it is an irrational and immoral act. If it fails the evidentialist's tests, then (on his own grounds) believing it is an irrational and immoral act. Either way, evidentialism is in big trouble.

Wise Christians therefore will not feel threatened when challenged to put up (that is, prove something) or shut up. They will respond to this challenge by demanding that the evidentialist put up or shut up. After all, it is the evidentialist who insists that it is irrational and immoral to believe anything without proof. There is no point in talking about Christianity's evidence until the evidentialist first produces the evidence for the thesis that underlies his challenge to the Christian.

The wise Christian will refuse to be backed into the

evidentialist's trap. He will not assume that his beliefs are substandard in some way unless he can first prove something. Such a Christian puts himself and his faith at a disadvantage. A person may be rational in holding certain beliefs, even if he cannot provide others with proofs that will satisfy them. A person may be within his epistemic rights in believing that God exists, even in the absence of supporting proofs and arguments.

Of course, none of this implies that Christians who reject evidentialism think that reason, evidence, and arguments are either irrelevant, unimportant or even unavailable.[31] Christians who reject evidentialism may do this without also thinking that theism lacks supporting reasons. Such believers may well think that plenty of arguments confirm their beliefs. They simply deny that their producing such arguments is a necessary condition for their act of holding those beliefs to be rational.

CONCLUSION

Our further examination of the test of reason has introduced us to complex but interesting and illuminating issues. The wise Christian will see reason, the laws of logic, as a friend of his worldview. As we have noted in this chapter, the test of reason creates embarrassing problems for a number of worldview beliefs that are held by enemies of theism. But possibly the test of reason is a two-edged sword. What should the Christian say about some of his beliefs that appear, perhaps only on first glance, to fail the test of reason? The answer to this question will occupy us in the next chapter.□

[31]There is much more that could be said about the question of evidentialism. For a more detailed discussion, see my *Faith and Reason*, chaps. 5-8.

Chapter 5

Christianity and the Test of Reason

It would be surprising if opponents of the Christian faith did not attempt to show that Christianity suffers from internal inconsistency. This is precisely what many have tried to do. Such attempts have taken a number of forms. In this chapter, I will examine two of the most common and important challenges the Christian faith faces in this regard.[1] In its first form, the accusation concerns the alleged inconsistency between what Christians believe about God and the troubling presence in God's creation of all kinds of evil. Anyone, the charge goes, who believes that an all-powerful, all-knowing, and all-loving God created a world with evil so pervasive is guilty somehow of believing a contradiction. In its second form, the challenger turns his attention to the Christian belief in the Incarnation. This, of course, is the belief that Jesus Christ is both fully God *and*

[1]The claim that Christianity contains contradictions assumes one other form, namely, that the very concept of God found in Christian theism is logically incoherent. Sometimes critics claim that the notion of an omnipotent God is logically inconsistent or that the concept of a Being who is both omniscient (all-knowing) and immutable (incapable of change) is incoherent. Because I have dealt with these issue in a separate book, *The Concept of God* (Grand Rapids: Zondervan, 1983), and because the debate often gets one into highly technical philosophical discussions, I will simply refer the reader to the other study.

fully man. If ever there was a contradiction, critics argue, that is it.

Both of these issues can get us into highly technical and tricky arguments. Since I am not writing this book for professional philosophers, I am determined to make the presentation accessible to nonspecialists. When necessary, I will refer the reader to more complete treatments where sophisticated ins and outs of problems are handled at a somewhat higher level. More advanced readers should keep my goal in view as they proceed.

THE DEDUCTIVE PROBLEM OF EVIL

The *deductive problem of evil* used to be a challenge that readers of philosophical literature encountered much more frequently than they now do. The reason this problem has largely disappeared from the literature is that a group of Christian philosophers, most notably Alvin Plantinga, has defused the issue.

The problem of evil rests on the easily recognized fact that several related and essential Christian beliefs about God appear to be incompatible with the fact of evil in the world. Christians believe that God is totally good, all-knowing, and all-powerful. We also believe that God created the world. The difficulties that these beliefs engender with respect to evil are obvious.

1. If God is good and loves all human beings, it is reasonable to believe that he wants to deliver the creatures he loves from evil and suffering.
2. If God is all-knowing, it is reasonable to believe that he knows how to deliver his creatures from evil and suffering.
3. If God is all-powerful, it is reasonable to believe that he is able to deliver his creatures from evil and suffering.

Given what Christians believe about God, it seems to follow that God wants to eliminate evil, that God knows how to eliminate evil, and that God has the power to eliminate evil. But evil exists. In fact, great amounts of evil exist. Indeed, great amounts of apparently senseless and purposeless evil exist. It seems reasonable to believe, then, that either God doesn't want to eliminate evil (casting doubt on his goodness) or doesn't know how to eliminate evil (raising questions about his knowledge) or lacks the power (raising questions about his almightiness). Troubled by their reflections on these difficulties, many have found it easy to take the additional step and conclude that the existence of evil in the world makes it unlikely that God exists.

Thinking Christians appear to be stuck between a rock and a hard place. They cannot deny the existence of evil, much of it gratuitous or meaningless. But as theists, questioning Christians must affirm their belief that this world despite all its evil was created by a good, loving, omnipotent, and omniscient God. The challenge for theists is to show that the existence of the evils we find in this world fits or is consistent with the Christian view of God and the world. In other words, what explanation can we offer of how the conceptual scheme that is the Christian worldview is consistent with the amount and kinds of evil we find in creation?

What I call the deductive version of the problem of evil attempts to show that the existence of evil is logically inconsistent with one or more major tenets of the Christian faith. Proponents of the deductive version claim that a logical contradiction lurks at the very core of Christian theism. The British philosopher J. L. Mackie, a deductive version advocate, in a 1955 article wrote, "It can be shown, not that religious beliefs lack rational support, but that they are positively irrational, that the several parts of the essential theological doctrine are *inconsistent* with one another."[2] Since a contradictory set of beliefs is necessarily

[2] J. L. Mackie, "Evil and Omnipotence," in *The Philosophy of Religion*, ed. Basil Mitchell (London: Oxford Univ. Press, 1971), 92. Mackie's article appeared originally in 1955 in the journal *Mind* (vol. 64).

false, the deductive version of the problem of evil would—
if sound—pose the most serious threat possible to Christian theism. It would mean that Christianity is not simply
possibly false, but necessarily false. Things can't get much
worse than that.

The problem arises because of a supposed contradiction that lies in the following six propositions:

1. God exists.
2. God is omnipotent.
3. God is omniscient.
4. God is omnibenevolent.
5. God created the world.
6. The world contains evil.

Obviously this list does not include two propositions,
one of which contradicts the other: *The world contains evil*
and *The world does not contain evil*. Since the list does not
include this pair of propositions, where is the alleged
contradiction? Critics of the Christian faith acknowledge
that nothing in this list *explicitly* contradicts another
premise. However, they argue that propositions 1–5 in
some way imply a seventh proposition, namely,

7. The world does not contain evil.

If that should prove to be true, then our set of Christian
beliefs (numbers 1–7) would indeed have a problem; the set
would be logically inconsistent.

However, in order to make their case, the critics must
find another proposition that in conjunction with statements 1–5 would imply proposition 7, the claim that the
world does not contain evil. Only by supplying such a
missing premise would the alleged contradiction become
evident. While proponents of the deductive problem of evil
tried every move possible, none of them succeeded. The
new propositions they offered to educe the sought-for
contradiction failed either because they were not true or
because they were not claims that Christians embrace. For
example, some anti-theists offered as the missing premise
the claim that an omnipotent being can do absolutely

anything, believing that when this proposition was added to our original list, it would require proposition seven, the claim that the world does not contain evil. In this way, they sought to generate the contradiction that would presumably demonstrate that Christian theism does contain a logical inconsistency at its core.

But there was a major catch to this move. The proposition is not true. Informed Christians have always recognized that an omnipotent being cannot do lots of things. For example, the Bible declares that God cannot lie or swear by a being greater than himself. The end result of all the hoopla over the alleged contradiction existing at the heart of the Christian faith turned out this way: no proponent of the deductive problem of evil ever succeeded in supplying the missing proposition needed to reveal the presumed contradiction.

Finally, Plantinga suggested a procedure by which Christians could demonstrate the logical consistency of their set of beliefs. Once done, this meant that Christians no longer needed to live in fear that an ingenious critic might produce the dreaded proposition that would confute their faith next week or next year. In formal logic, once the logical consistency of a set of propositions has been demonstrated, it then becomes impossible ever to uncover an inconsistency in the set.

All that is required to prove our list of propositions is logically consistent (and thus forever immune to the possibility of being shown to be inconsistent) is to add a new proposition that is logically possible, which means simply that it does not describe a contradictory state of affairs. The new proposition must be consistent with the other propositions in the list, and, in conjunction with the other propositions, it must entail that evil exists in the world. The proposition that Plantinga proposed was the claim that *God creates a world that now contains evil and has a good reason for doing so.*

Telescoping our earlier list to save space, our new list of Christian beliefs looks like this:

1. God exists, is omnipotent, omnibenevolent, and created the world.
2. God created a world that now contains evil and had a good reason for doing so.
3. Therefore, the world contains evil.

Numbers 1 and 2 taken together do, of course, entail 3. Therefore, the propositions from our original list of Christian beliefs that now appear in number 1 are logically consistent with the existence of evil. The only relevant question regarding proposition 2 is whether it is possibly true. Obviously it is since it is not logically false (is not a contradiction). Therefore, our original list of Christian beliefs is shown to be logically consistent, from which it follows that the deductive problem of evil has been answered. The existence of evil in the world cannot be used to demonstrate a logical inconsistency at the heart of Christian belief.

The preceding discussion has of necessity skipped over a number of details, many of them technical in nature. The interested reader is advised to examine these details in other publications, which are readily available.[3] But the point is clear. The existence of evil in the world does not create a problem of logic for the Christian. Of course, it may still raise other sorts of problems, which we will examine in a later chapter. It is important to note that even J. L. Mackie, one of the fathers of the deductive problem of evil whom I cited earlier, conceded that his scheme "does not, after all, show that the central doctrines of theism are logically inconsistent with one another."[4] Another philosopher, a frequent critic of Christian theism, William Rowe, admits, "Some philosophers have contended that the existence of evil is *logically inconsistent* with the existence of the theistic God. No one, I think, has succeeded in establishing such an extravagant claim. Indeed [granted the

[3]See, for example, my *Faith and Reason*, chap. 13.
[4]J. L. Mackie, *The Miracle of Theism* (Oxford: Clarendon Press, 1982), 154.

belief that humans possess the power to make undetermined choices], there is a fairly compelling argument for the view that the existence of evil is logically consistent with the theistic God."[5]

We may ask, "But why did God permit evil?" However, the relevant issue here is that such a reason need not be known or produced for the argument of this section to succeed. The rules of modern logic make the strategy of this argument successful, whether or not we can identify God's reason. The only necessity at the moment is that the claim that God has a reason for creating a world that now contains evil is logically possible. Since it is, the argument succeeds and the attempt to locate a contradiction at the heart of Christian theism fails.[6]

As a final observation, we should note that nothing significant follows from the fact that Christians may admit they don't know God's reason for permitting evil. Some opponents of Christianity act as though such an admission implies that there is no reason. This hardly follows. In fact, all one could reasonably infer from the admission is that the human being in question does not know everything. But that is hardly surprising news.

THE INCARNATION

Christians use the word *incarnation* to express their belief that the birth of Jesus Christ marked the entrance of the eternal and divine Son of God into the human race. The Incarnation is an essential Christian belief. If this doctrine is false, the Christian faith is false. Correct thinking about Jesus Christ diminishes neither his full and complete humanity nor his full and complete deity. Jesus Christ is

[5]William L. Rowe, "The Problem of Evil and Some Varieties of Atheism," *American Philosophical Quarterly* 16 (1979): 335.
[6]Once again, I recognize how readers untrained in logic may have difficulty following what has gone on in the past few pages. For that reason, I refer them again to the more detailed treatment of the subject in my *Faith and Reason*, chap. 13.

God; let there be no mistake about this. But he is also human. Any wavering with regard to either claim results in a defective Christology and a heretical faith.

We are not surprised, therefore, when opponents of the historic Christian faith take aim at this core doctrine. The Incarnation is an inviting target, not only because it is a central belief, but also because it seems susceptible to the charge that this is one point where Christians do believe a logical contradiction.

The argument sets up as follows: the Christian God possesses attributes like omnipotence, omniscience, incorporeality, and sinlessness. God also exists necessarily, which means, among other things, that there can be neither beginning nor end to his existence. Moreover, these properties belong to God essentially or necessarily, which is to say that if God were to lose any of his essential properties he would cease to be God. A being simply cannot be God if he lacks omnipotence, omniscience, and the like.

But when we reflect on the nature of humanness, we seem to encounter a creature with precisely the opposite properties. Human beings are, as we know, *not* omnipotent, omniscient, incorporeal (spiritual), or sinless. Nor do we exist necessarily. Our existence is contingent, that is, dependent on many things other than ourselves. Given these seemingly obvious incompatibilities between God and man, how could any being possibly be both God and man? In a 1988 article in *The Asbury Theological Journal*, Thomas V. Morris, University of Notre Dame philosopher, summarizes the problem:

> Jesus is claimed in the doctrine of the Incarnation to have been both fully human and fully divine. But it is logically impossible for any being to exemplify at one and the same time both a property and its logical complement [7]. Thus, recent critics have concluded, it

[7] I hope the reader will remember the discussion in chapter four of the law of noncontradiction, that a thing cannot possess a property (*B*) and the complement of that property (non-*B*) at the same time in the same sense.

is logically impossible for any one person to be both human and divine, to have all the attributes proper to deity and all those ingredient in human nature as well. The doctrine of the Incarnation on this view is an incoherent theological development of the early church which must be discarded by us in favor of some other way of conceptualizing the importance of Jesus for Christian faith. He could not possibly have been God Incarnate, a literally divine person in human nature.[8]

This is a serious difficulty. As we will see, developing an appropriate response to this challenge will require hard thinking about complex issues. But since the challenge is too serious to ignore, the task must be done.

In his lengthy, detailed, and technical book *The Logic of God Incarnate*,[9] Morris has produced one of the better approaches to this problem. Fortunately, he has also presented his argument in more popular form in *The Asbury Theological Journal* article cited above. My own treatment will follow Morris's lead. I hope that many readers will examine Morris's more detailed presentation in his book.

According to Morris, we can work our way out of this problem if we first understand and then properly apply three major distinctions, namely,

1. The distinction between essential and nonessential properties
2. The distinction between essential and common properties, and
3. The distinction between being *fully* human and *merely* human.

While the terminology may seem intimidating, the basic points are not that hard to grasp.

[8]Thomas V. Morris, "Understanding God Incarnate," *The Asbury Theological Journal* 43 (1988), 64 65.
[9]Thomas V. Morris, *The Logic of God Incarnate* (Ithaca: Cornell Univ. Press, 1986).

Essential and Nonessential Properties

The word *property* refers to any feature or characteristic of something. In any proposition of the form *S* is *P*, the predicate of the proposition is one way we have of marking off the properties of things. Consider the properties we can attribute to Socrates simply by filling in the blank in the following sentence: "Socrates is _____." All of the following terms denote properties or traits or characteristics of Socrates: "bald," "citizen of Athens," "honorable," "short," "the husband of Xanthippe," and so on. Everything has properties and one way we refer to those properties is by using them as predicates applied to a given subject.

With this out of the way, the next step is to recognize that properties are of two different types, essential and nonessential. Consider as an example a red ball. The color of the object is nonessential in the sense that if we somehow changed the color to yellow or green, the object would still be a ball. But when we're dealing with a ball, the property of roundness is an essential property. You can't have a ball that isn't round. If you change this feature of our object, it is no longer a ball.

Put in its simplest terms, an essential property is one that cannot be changed or lost without the object in question ceasing to be the *kind* of thing it is. Things belong to classes or sets. In order to be a member of the class of all balls, everything within that set must possess the property of roundness. Roundness, then, is an essential property of being a ball. When anything that once was a member of the class of all balls loses its roundness, it also loses its membership in that set.

A number of properties are essential to being God. They include at least the following: necessary existence, omnipotence, omniscience, sinlessness, and so on. Any being lacking these and the other essential properties of deity could *not* be God. Obviously, then, when Christians affirm that Jesus is God, they are also affirming that Jesus possesses eternally and necessarily all of the essential properties of God. This much is easy.

Matters become difficult when we start trying to identify the essential properties of a human being. Aristotle thought that rationality (being a thinking and reasoning being) was an essential property of humans. Rationality certainly seems to be one property among others that make up the essence of a human being, that sets humans apart from other creatures on our planet.

Where the critic goes wrong, I contend, is in his belief that such properties as *lacking omnipotence, lacking omniscience, lacking sinlessness* are also essential in some way to being a human being. But in order to see the next step in our argument, it will be necessary first to introduce the distinction between essential properties and common properties.

Essential and Common Properties

What Morris calls common properties are often mistakenly thought of as essential properties. This error lies at the foundation of the confused thinking that leads some to think the doctrine of the Incarnation entails a contradiction. A common property is any property that human beings typically possess without also being essential. As an example of a common property, Morris refers to the property of having ten fingers. Since almost every human being has ten fingers, it is common to humanity. But clearly, having ten fingers is not essential to being a human being. A human can lose one or even ten fingers and *still be a human being.* Hence, the common property of having ten fingers is not an essential property. Likewise, we could say that living on earth is a common human property. But it is conceivable that at some time in the future, some humans will be born and live out their entire lives on other planets. And so once again, a property that we have found common to all men turns out not to be essential.

Having made these points, Morris then explains the relevance of his two distinctions to the doctrine of the Incarnation:

> It is certainly quite common for human beings to lack omnipotence, omniscience, necessary existence, and so on. I think any orthodox Christian will agree that, apart from Jesus, these are even universal features of human existence. Further, in the case of any of us who do exemplify the logical complements of these distinctively divine attributes, it may well be most reasonable to hold that they are in our case essential attributes. I, for example, could not possibly become omnipotent. As a creature, I am essentially limited in power. But why think this is true on account of *human nature*? Why think that any attributes incompatible with deity are elements of human nature, properties without which one could not be truly or fully human?[10]

In other words, even if I and every other human person—other than Jesus—is characterized by the complements of such divine properties as omnipotence and omniscience, where is the argument that shows that these limitations are somehow essential to my being human? Possibly, these limitations are only common human properties, not essential ones.

Being *Fully* Human and Being *Merely* Human

The best place to begin this point is with Morris's explanation. "An individual is *fully human*," he writes, "[in any case where] that individual has all essential human properties, all the properties composing basic human nature. An individual is *merely human* if he has all those properties *plus* some additional limitation properties as well, properties such as that of lacking omnipotence, that of lacking omniscience, and so on."[11]

[10]Morris, "Understanding God Incarnate," 66.
[11]Ibid.

Now, Morris adds, what orthodox Christians insist upon is the claim that "Jesus was fully human without being merely human."[12] This means two things: first, that Jesus possessed *all* the properties that are essential to being a human being. And second, that Jesus also possessed all the properties that are essential to deity. The properties that the critic makes so much of (such as lacking omniscience) and insists are essential to being a human being are simply dealt with, Morris argues, in a confused way.

Once Christians arm themselves with the distinctions noted above, they are equipped to counter the critic's accusation that orthodox Christology is self-contradictory. What the orthodox understanding of the Incarnation expresses are the claims that: (1) Jesus Christ is fully God, that is, he possesses all of the essential attributes or properties of God; (2) Jesus Christ is also fully human, that is, he possesses all of the essential properties of a human being, none of which turn out to be the limiting properties that weigh so heavily in the argument of the critic, such as lacking omniscience; and (3) Jesus Christ was not merely human, that is, he did not possess any of the limitation properties we have noted that are in fact complements of the divine attributes.

Once these distinctions are applied to the alleged contradiction that Christian opponents claim exists in the Incarnation, the contradiction disappears. If this were a book in systematic or philosophical theology, we might wish to pursue other interesting questions about this aspect of historic Christianity's understanding of the two natures of Christ. I have met the limited objectives of this chapter and will not attempt the rest of that task here. For those interested in going further, Tom Morris's studies are a profitable place to begin.

[12]Ibid.

CONCLUSION

Given the importance this book has attached to the laws of logic as a test of worldviews, it would have been inappropriate for me to ignore the more prominent challenges to the logical coherence of the Christian worldview. But once I accepted the challenges, I bumped into the problem of handling these issues in a responsible way without at the same time allowing the discussion to become too deeply mired in philosophical technicalities. I have had to walk a fine line, trying to handle the issues responsibly while at the same time making my discussion simple enough for nonspecialists to follow the argument. I hope that I succeeded with the majority of my readers.

At first encounter, the two issues central to this chapter can give untrained Christians a great deal of trouble. And, of course, if one really begins to think that Christianity is self-contradictory on this or that matter, the personal results can be devastating. Once we learn to sort things out, however, it soon becomes apparent that no logical problem exists. Neither the Incarnation nor the problem of evil points to a genuine contradiction at the center of the Christian faith.

But as we all know, one thing often leads to another. My treatment of the problem of evil in this chapter dealt exclusively with the question of whether the existence of evil in God's creation is logically inconsistent with the creator of that world being all-powerful, all-good, and all-knowing. In the chapter that follows, I investigate a far more potent version of the problem of evil that turns out to be the most serious threat to the rational believability of the Christian worldview.□

Chapter 6

A Further Look at the Problem of Evil

In chapter 5, we noticed the concession of two prominent critics of Christianity that the deductive problem of evil should be judged a failure. Given the work of philosophers like Alvin Plantinga, the existence of evil in the world cannot be shown to be logically incompatible with other essential Christian beliefs about the nature and actions of God. It is simply not true that, because of evil, Christian theism is self-contradictory and hence necessarily false.

But the shortcomings of the deductive problem of evil do not mean that opponents of Christian theism have given up on the problem of evil. It simply means that they have turned to a different way of formulating the problem. The move from the discredited deductive to an inductive form of the problem of evil is a shift from the strong claim that theism is logically false to the more modest assertion that it is probably false. According to advocates of the inductive problem of evil, evil tips the scales of probability against theism; the existence of evil makes theistic belief improbable or implausible.

Most attempts to answer the problem of evil are variations on one basic theme, namely, that God permits evil either to make possible some greater good or to avoid some greater evil. God, it is claimed, always has some reason for allowing evil. At this point, some theists stop and admit that they simply do not know what God's reasons are. Lest anyone dismiss this procedure too quickly, we should ask what, if anything, follows from a Christian's admission that he doesn't know God's reason for permitting evil. According to Plantinga, "Very little of interest. Why suppose that if God *does* have a good reason for permitting evil, the theist would be the first to know? Perhaps God has a good reason, but that reason is too complicated for us to understand. Or perhaps He has not revealed it for some other reason. The fact that the theist doesn't know why God permits evil is, perhaps, an interesting fact about the theist, but by itself it shows little or nothing relevant to the rationality of belief in God."[1] There would be nothing philosophically substandard about just leaving the entire matter right here.

However, many Christian thinkers have been brave (and possibly foolish) enough to offer suggestions as to what God's reasons for permitting evil might be. Some have appealed to the value and importance of human free will. It is certainly easy to see how much of the evil in the world results from human choices. It is also worthwhile to reflect on the logical consequences that would follow any denial of significant moral freedom to humans. Is there not a sense in which some degree of free choice is a condition for divinely approved dispositions such as love and kindness? What if it should be impossible to do anything pleasing to God without power of choice? If choice is a condition for doing good, is it not also a condition for doing acts of moral evil? The whole area of human choice is sticky, both philosophically and theologically. Hence, some are reluctant to push arguments too far. But at least there is a *prima facie* case for believing that God would have good reasons for creating humans with significant moral freedom. If so, then it is

[1]Alvin Plantinga, *God, Freedom and Evil* (Grand Rapids: Eerdmans, 1974), 10.

hard to see how we can dismiss this same freedom as the cause of the moral evil that abounds in the world.

Other Christians draw attention to the importance of humans living in an orderly universe governed by law as a plausible reasons for some kinds of evil. One such thinker was the British philosopher F. R. Tennant, who wrote:

> It cannot be too strongly insisted that a world which is to be a moral order must be a physical order character- ized by law or regularity. . . . Without such regularity in physical phenomena there could be no probability to guide us: no prediction, no prudence, no accumulation of ordered experience, no pursuit of premeditated ends, no formation of habit, no possibility of character or of culture. Our intellectual faculties could not have developed. . . And without rationality, morality is impossible.[2]

Clearly we live in a universe that exhibits order, an order expressed in the laws of nature described by the appropriate science. Moral freedom could not exist apart from such an orderly environment. If the world were totally unpredictable, if we could never know from one moment to the next, what to expect from nature, both science and meaningful moral conduct would be impossible. But if nature sets the stage for moral good, it does the same for moral evil. One reason people can be held accountable when they pull the trigger of a loaded gun is the predictabil- ity of what will follow that action.

Just as a regular natural order is a necessary condition for moral good and moral evil, it also must function in any account of natural evil, evil that does not result from human action. Michael Peterson notes, "That same water which sustains and refreshes can also drown; the same drug which relieves suffering can cause crippling psychological addiction; the same sun which gives light and life can parch fields and bring famine; the same neural arrangements

[2]F. R. Tennant, *Philosophical Theology* (New York: Cambridge Univ. Press, 1928), 2:199–200.

which transmit intense pleasure and ecstasy can also bring extreme pain and agony."[3]

Many human complaints about the occurrence of specific natural evils such as floods, earthquakes, or tornadoes seem to be expressions of a desire that—at least in that instance—the natural order of things had been suspended or different somehow. If it makes sense to believe that God created the universe with the kind of regularity and order that makes the formulation of laws of science possible, if it makes sense to think that this kind of orderly universe would be better overall than a chaotic and unpredictable universe, we might be wise to think twice before cursing some particular outcome of that order.

Certainly much more could be said about the role that natural order plays in efforts to ease the problem of evil.[4] Nothing that has been said implies we must regard the present world as the best possible world or the only possible world. The point is simply that unless there is some natural order, important goods like moral freedom cannot exist. And there seems to be good reason to believe that without a world order like our present one, we could not have the good things so familiar to us. No matter what the laws of nature might have been, there would have been unpleasant side effects so long as they operated as *laws*.

A third popular approach to God's possible reasons for allowing evil appeals to the notion of soul making. According to this view, in order for God to produce the virtuous beings with whom he wants fellowship, these individuals must face challenges that teach them the intrinsic worth of the virtues God possesses perfectly. Virtues cannot be created instantaneously; the process by which they are acquired is part of the nature of having them. Human beings cannot grow in an environment that is free of risk and danger and disappointment. God, it appears, had good

[3]Michael Peterson, *Evil and the Christian God* (Grand Rapids: Baker, 1982), 111.
[4]For a discussion of alleged problems with this line of thinking, see my *Faith and Reason*, 201–4.

reasons for placing us in an environment that challenges and tests us.

Most of what we consider significant with regard to human spiritual and moral development arises as a result of interaction with challenge. An athlete cannot accomplish his best without sacrifice, effort, training, and struggle. Human spiritual and moral growth also arises out of a struggle against various kinds of challenge. As Richard Purtill explains, "To be able to play like Heifetz, or philosophize like Wittgenstein, is not really separable from the long years of practice and playing, or the long years of wrestling with philosophical problems. But even if the end result could be achieved without pain, it would thereby be less valuable."[5] We cannot live in a plastic environment that bends to our every desire, in which we get everything we want. That environment would stifle growth and development.[6]

THE PROBLEM OF GRATUITOUS EVIL

The responses to the problem of evil noted thus far are all versions of an appeal to greater good; they involve the claim that God permits evil because it is a necessary condition for the attainment of some greater good or the avoidance of some greater evil. But what if the world contains gratuitous evil, that is, truly senseless, mindless, irrational, and meaningless evil? If this is true, the appeal to greater good would collapse and with it, apparently, would also fall the kinds of arguments we have noticed.

One version of the problem of gratuitous evil reasons in the following way:

1. If God exists, then all evil has a justifying reason.

[5]Richard L. Purtill, *Reason to Believe* (Grand Rapids: Eerdmans, 1974), 57.
[6]Once again the need to cover other subjects makes it necessary to cut off a discussion while there is still more to say. For a more complete treatment of the appeal to soul making, see my *Faith and Reason*, 204–8.

2. But it is not the case that all evil has a justifying reason.[7]
3. Therefore, God does not exist.

What can we say about this argument? To begin with, it is certainly valid; it conforms to the rules of formal logic. If the premises are true, then the conclusion is certainly true. But are the premises true? Suppose for now we concentrate only on the second premise, the claim that not all evil has a justifying reason. We can ask several questions about this claim. For one thing, how does the critic of Christian theism know that premise 2 is true? And to get right to the heart of the matter, how could any human being know that gratuitous evil exists? Any sensitive and observant person must admit that many evils that *appear* to be gratuitous pervade the world: accidents that strike people down in the prime of life, diseases that result in long periods of horrible suffering, birth defects, natural disasters that can suddenly kill hundreds of people and destroy the lives of survivors. But given the limitations of human knowledge, it is hard to see how any human being could actually *know* that a specific instance of evil really is gratuitous. In fact, it looks as though a person would have to be omniscient in order to *know* that some particular evil is totally senseless and purposeless.

It seems, then, the most any human can claim to know is that evil that *appears* gratuitous is present. But of course such a claim in the place of premise 2 would not entail the conclusion.

Jane Mary Trau has provided a different formulation of the inductive problem of evil. She writes:

> It seems that unless it can be shown that all cases of apparent gratuitous suffering are in fact not purposeless, it is most reasonable to believe that they are as they appear to be; and since it cannot be shown that they are in fact not purposeless, it is reasonable to

[7]This premise is simply another way of saying that the world contains gratuitous evil.

believe that they are as they appear to be; since there appear to be such cases it is more reasonable to believe that God does not exist.[8]

Trau, as she later makes clear, does not accept this argument; she presents it only as a version of the inductive problem of evil. Her response to the argument is instructive. The second premise of the argument involves an appeal to ignorance, a common logical fallacy, she points out. Simply because the theist cannot prove that all evils in the world are not gratuitous, it hardly follows that some of them are. Indeed, Trau goes on to say:

> . . . the most reasonable position to hold appears to be this: we cannot explain cases of apparently gratuitous suffering until we know whether or not they are indeed gratuitous. And this we can never claim unless we are sure as to the ontological status of God [that is, does God exist?]. Since we cannot prove or disprove His non-existence [via the argument from gratuitous evil], we must first prove or disprove His existence. Until that is accomplished we cannot know whether there are such cases.[9]

According to Trau, the one sure way of showing that the world does contain gratuitous evils is to prove that God does not exist. But it would then seem to follow that one cannot appeal to gratuitous evils while arguing against the existence of God—unless, that is, one is unconcerned about begging the question.

THE PROBLEM OF EVIL AND NON-CHRISTIAN WORLDVIEWS

Every opponent of historic Christianity, it seems, raises the problem of evil as a way of challenging the Christian belief in God. But it is worth considering whether

---

[8]Jane Mary Trau, "Fallacies in the Argument from Gratuitous Suffering," *The New Scholasticism* 60 (1986), 487–88.
[9]Ibid., 489.

there are competing worldviews out there that have no logical right to appeal to this issue. In the next chapter, for example, we will be examining the worldview known as naturalism. One of the things we'll learn about naturalism is that none of its adherents is logically justified in believing in any objective good.[10] "Good" and "evil" in a naturalistic universe cannot possibly refer to anything transcendent, anything that has standing outside of the natural order of things. For this reason, many naturalists simply say that what we call good and evil are merely subjective preferences. While other naturalists balk at this extreme and problematic view, they seem obliged nonetheless to treat good and evil as relative.

The interesting point here is that few naturalists seem to have realized how their relativist approach to good and evil disqualifies them logically from being advocates of the problem of evil. Whenever they seek to embarrass Christians by describing a given evil, they do so in terms that simply are not consistent with their naturalistic understanding of things.

A similar problem seems to exist for pantheistic opponents of Christianity. The people I have especially in mind at this point are advocates of what is sometimes called New Age thinking. But it would also be a problem for other types of pantheists, including adherents of some Eastern religions. The problem for the pantheist is this: If everything is one, that is, part of one wholistic system, then the One or God (or whatever it is called) ends up being above good and evil. In fact, what we see as good and evil are really the result of an illusion or an improper way of "seeing" things. One may wonder how anyone influenced by pantheism can consistently hurl at Christians the challenge of the problem of evil.

It looks as though the only people who can consistently wrestle with the problem of evil are people, like

---

[10]Indeed, as I will argue in the next chapter, no proponent of naturalism is *logically justified* in believing any proposition to be true.

Christians, who believe that good and evil are neither relative nor illusory. It certainly appears that many advocates of non-Christian worldviews are guilty of inconsistencies when they talk about evil in the way they must talk for any problem of evil to exist.

CONCLUSION

The last thing I want to do is leave the reader with the impression that I do not take the problem of evil seriously. It would be hard to think of a more serious threat to the rationality of Christian belief.

But in spite of the formidable issues raised by the problem of evil, they do not invalidate the claim that the Christian worldview is a rational, believable option. Evil *is* a problem, and no one should be foolish enough to think it isn't. But the Christian worldview has the resources to deal with the theoretical problem. And, as we have suggested, opponents of Christianity who eagerly and gleefully throw this issue into the face of Christians need to pay more attention to difficulties that follow from the incoherence their theories introduce into their worldviews.□

Chapter 7

Naturalism

The major competition to the Christian worldview in the part of the world normally thought of as Christendom is a system that often goes by the name of naturalism. The touchstone proposition or basic presupposition of naturalism states: "Nothing exists outside the material, mechanical (that is, nonpurposeful), natural order." S. D. Gaede explains:

> The naturalistic world view rests upon the belief that the material universe is the sum total of reality. To put it negatively, naturalism holds to the proposition that the supernatural, in any form, does not exist. . . . The naturalistic world view assumes that the matter or stuff which makes up the universe has never been created but has always existed. This is because an act of creation presupposes the existence of some reality outside of, or larger than, the world order—incompatible with the tenet that the material universe is the sum total of reality. Naturalism normally assumes that always-existing matter has developed into the ordered universe which we see by a blind, timeless process of chance. The human being, as one part of the natural universe, is also the result of matter, time, and chance. Within the context of the naturalistic world

view, miracles, as such, do not exist; they are natural events which have yet to be explained.[1]

In his book *Miracles*, C. S. Lewis brilliantly showed that most Westerners who object to the Christian belief in miracles do so because they have made a prior commitment to the naturalistic worldview. In that book, Lewis says of naturalism:

What the Naturalist believes is that the ultimate Fact, the thing you can't go behind, is a vast process in space and time which is *going on of its own accord*. Inside that total system every particular event (such as your sitting reading this book) happens because some other event has happened; in the long run, because the Total Event is happening. Each particular thing (such as this page) is what it is because other things are what they are; and so, eventually, because the whole system is what it is. All the things and events are so completely interlocked that no one of them can claim the slightest independence from "the whole show." None of them exists "on its own" or "goes on of its own accord" except in the sense that it exhibits at some particular place and time, that general "existence on its own" or "behaviour of its own accord" which belongs to "Nature" (the great total interlocked event) as a whole. Thus no thoroughgoing Naturalist believes in free will: for free will would mean that human beings have the power of independent action, the power of doing something more or other than what was involved by the total series of events. And any such separate power of originating events is what the Naturalist denies. Spontaneity, originality, action "on its own," is a privilege reserved for "the whole show," which he calls *Nature*.[2]

For a naturalist, the universe is analogous to a box. Everything that happens inside the box (the natural order) is

[1]S. D. Gaede, *Where Gods May Dwell* (Grand Rapids: Eerdmans, 1985), 35.
[2]C. S. Lewis, *Miracles* (New York: Macmillan, 1960), 6–7.

caused by or is explicable in terms of other things that exist within the box. *Nothing* (including God) exists outside the box; therefore, nothing outside the box we call the universe or nature can have any causal effect within the box. A picture representing naturalism would look like this:

NOTHING

THE NATURAL ORDER

It is important to notice that the box (the natural order) is closed. Even if something did exist outside the box, it could not possibly serve as the cause of anything that happened within the box. *Everything* that happens within nature has its cause in something else that exists within the box. Philosopher William Halverson explains:

> Naturalism asserts . . . that what happens in the world is theoretically explicable without residue in terms of the internal structures and the external relations of these material entities. The world is . . . like a gigantic machine whose parts are so numerous and whose processes are so complex that we have thus far been able to achieve only a very partial and fragmentary understanding of how it works. In principle, however, everything that occurs is ultimately explicable in terms of the properties and relations of the particles of which matter is composed. Once again the point may be stated simply: determinism is true.[3]

A naturalist, then, is someone who believes (or who would believe if he or she were consistent) the following propositions:

1. Only nature exists. By *nature*, I mean (following Stephen Davis) "the sum total of what could in principle be observed by human beings or be studied by methods

[3]William H. Halverson, *A Concise Introduction to Philosophy*, 3d ed. (New York: Random House, 1976), 394.

analogous to those used in the natural sciences."[4] For anyone who thinks in terms of a naturalistic worldview, God does not exist since by definition, if anything does exist, it is part of the box.

2. Nature has always existed. It would be inconsistent for any naturalist to believe in the Christian doctrine of creation. As Halverson explains, "Theism says, 'In the beginning, God'; naturalism says, 'In the beginning matter.'"[5] There never was a time when the natural order did not exist. Nature does not depend upon anything else for its existence.

3. Nature is characterized by total uniformity. The regularity of nature precludes the occurrence of anything like a miracle. Miracles are impossible because there is nothing outside the box that would bring about any occurrence within nature. But miracles are impossible also because the regularity and uniformity of the natural order precludes the occurrence of any irregular event.

4. Nature is a deterministic system. The belief in free will presupposes a theory of human agency whereby human beings acting apart from any totally determining causes can themselves function as causes in the natural order. That belief is incompatible with the presuppositions of naturalism.

5. Nature is a materialistic system. "Naturalism asserts," Halverson writes, "that the primary constituents of reality are material entities. By this I do not mean that only material entities exist; I am not denying the reality— the real existence—of such things as hopes, plans, behavior, language, logical inferences, and so on. What I am asserting, however, is that anything that is real is, in the last analysis, explicable as a material entity or as a form or function or action of a material entity."[6] Whatever such things as thoughts, beliefs, and inferences are, they are

[4]Stephen T. Davis, "Is It Possible To Know That Jesus Was Raised From the Dead?" *Faith and Philosophy* (1984), 154.
[5]Halverson, *A Concise Introduction to Philosophy*, 394.
[6]Ibid.

either material things or reducible to or explainable in terms of material things or caused by something material.

6. Nature is a self-explanatory system. Any and every thing that happens within the natural order must, at least in principle, be explainable in terms of other elements of the natural order. It is never necessary to seek the explanation for any event within nature in something beyond the natural order.

Clearly, any person under the control of naturalistic presuppositions could not consistently believe in the miraculous. For such a person, evidence of putative miracles can never be persuasive. Miracles, by definition, are impossible. No arguments on behalf of the miraculous can possibly succeed with a naturalist. The only proper way to address that unbelief is to *begin* by challenging his or her naturalism.

We must note one thing more about naturalism. The Christian should not allow the naturalist the self-deception that the steps by which he came to believe in naturalism are somehow superior to or, for that matter, even different from the manner in which the Christian came to adopt the theistic worldview. It is simply not true that "Science" somehow compels open-minded, intellectually superior people to become naturalists. There is no more "proof" to support naturalism than that which supports theism. It is important to help the naturalist recognize that in an important sense his choice of naturalism is a *religious* act, an act of the heart that relates to his ultimate concerns.

What are the more important ways the Christian worldview differs from naturalism? The following picture of the Christian worldview is a good place to start.

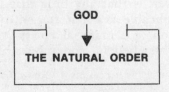

GOD

THE NATURAL ORDER

This diagram illustrates three important elements of the Christian worldview:

1. God exists outside the box.
2. God created the box.
3. God acts causally within the box.

Christian theism, then, rejects the naturalist's contention that nothing, including God, exists outside of the natural order. It also denies the eternity of nature. God created the world freely and *ex nihilo*. The universe is contingent in the sense that it could not have begun to exist without God's creative act and it could not continue to exist without God's sustaining activity.

It is especially important to note that aside from the fact that the box is "open" to causes existing outside the box, the Christian's scientific understanding of the natural order need not differ in any way from that of the naturalist. Christians believe that nature exhibits patterns of order and regularity. Of course, they also believe that this uniformity results from God's free decision to create the universe in a particular way. Christian theism recognizes the same cause-and-effect order within the natural order as does the naturalist. But the Christian believes that the natural order depends on God for both its existence and its order. When the Christian asserts that God is capable of exerting causal influence within the natural order, he does not mean necessarily that such divine action results in a suspension or violation of the natural order.[7] The essential point is that the world is not closed to God's causal activity.

Finally, Christian theism denies that nature is a self-explanatory system. The very existence of the contingent universe requires that we seek the cause of its being in a necessary being, one that does not depend upon anything else for its existence. Laws operating within the natural

---

[7]This touches on a complex issue that I do not have time to pursue in this book, namely, whether miracles must be viewed as violations of the laws of nature. In another book, I counsel that this is an unwise position. See my *Faith and Reason*, chaps. 16–17.

order owe their existence to God's creative activity. And many things that happen within the natural order are affected by or influenced by or brought about by free acts of the personal God.

THE CASE AGAINST NATURALISM

A careful analysis of naturalism reveals a problem so serious that it fails one of the major tests that rational men and women will expect any worldview to pass. In order to see how this is so, it is necessary first to recall that naturalism regards the universe as a self-contained and self-explanatory system. There is nothing outside the box we call nature that can explain or that is necessary to explain anything inside the box. Naturalism claims that *everything* can be explained in terms of something else within the natural order. This dogma is not an accidental or nonessential feature of the naturalistic position. All that is required for naturalism to be false is the discovery of one thing that cannot be explained in the naturalistic way. C. S. Lewis set up this line of argument:

> If necessities of thought force us to allow to any one thing any degree of independence from the Total System—if any one thing makes good a claim to be on its own, to be something more than an expression of the character of Nature as a whole—then we have abandoned Naturalism. For by Naturalism we mean the doctrine that only Nature—the whole interlocked system—exists. And if that were true, every thing and event would, if we knew enough, be explicable without remainder ... as a necessary product of the system.[8]

[8]Lewis, *Miracles*, 12. Lewis experts will note that I am following his argument in the second edition of the book. The first edition contained an argument against naturalism that Lewis came to see as fallacious.

With a little effort, we can quickly see that no thoughtful naturalist can ignore at least one thing. Lewis explains:

> All possible knowledge . . . depends on the validity of reasoning. If the feeling of certainty which we express by words like *must be* and *therefore* and *since* is a real perception of how things outside our own minds really "must" be, well and good. But if this certainty is merely a feeling *in* our minds and not a genuine insight into realities beyond them—if it merely represents the ways our minds happen to work—then we have no knowledge. Unless human reasoning is valid no science can be true.[9]

The human mind, as we know, has the power to grasp contingent truth, that is, whatever *is* the case. But the human mind also has the power to grasp *necessary connections*, that is, what *must* be the case. This latter power, the ability to grasp *necessary* connections, is the essential feature of human *reasoning*. If it is true that all men are mortal and if it is true that Socrates is a man, then it *must* be true that Socrates is mortal.

Naturalists must appeal to this kind of necessary connection in their arguments for naturalism; indeed, in their reasoning about everything. But can naturalists account for this essential element of the reasoning process that they utilize in their arguments for their own position? Lewis thinks not. As Lewis sees it, naturalism "discredits our processes of reasoning or at least reduces their credit to such a humble level that it can no longer support Naturalism itself."[10] Lewis argues:

> It follows that no account of the universe [including naturalism] can be true unless that account leaves it possible for our thinking to be a real insight. A theory which explained everything else in the whole universe but which made it impossible to believe that our

[9]Ibid., 14.
[10]Ibid., 15.

123

thinking was valid, would be utterly out of court. For that theory would itself have been reached by thinking, and if thinking is not valid that theory would, of course, be itself demolished. It would have destroyed its own credentials. It would be an argument which proved that no argument was sound—a proof that there are no such things as proofs—which is nonsense.[11]

Lewis is careful to point out that his argument is *not* grounded on the claim that naturalism affirms every human judgment (like every event in the universe) has a cause. He knows that even though my belief about a matter may be caused by nonrational factors, my belief may still be true.[12] In the argument before us, Lewis is talking about something else, namely, the logical connection between a belief and the ground of that belief. It is one thing for a belief to have a nonrational cause; it is something else for a belief to have a reason or ground. The ravings of a madman may have a cause but lack any justifying ground. The reasoning of a philosopher may also have a cause but possess a justifying ground.[13] What naturalism does, according to Lewis, is sever what should be unseverable, the link between conclusions and the grounds or reasons for those conclusions. As Lewis says, "Unless our conclusion is the logical consequent from a ground it will be worthless [as an example of a *reasoned* conclusion] and could be true only by a fluke."[14] Therefore, naturalism "offers what professes to be a full account of our mental behaviour; but this account on

[11]Ibid., 14–15.

[12]The kind of argument Lewis rejects here is similar to the fallacious argument he himself had advanced (and later rejected) in the first edition of *Miracles*.

[13]For example, a person suffering from a particular form of mental illness might believe something because he "hears" an inner voice. We tend to judge such people as mad when their conclusions lack any justifying ground. The beliefs of the philosopher I describe may also have a cause, e.g., something that happened in the philosopher's childhood perhaps. One would hope that a person aspiring to the title of philosopher would be able to produce grounds for his beliefs.

[14]Lewis, *Miracles*, 16.

inspection, leaves no room for the acts of knowing or insight on which the whole value of our thinking, as a means to truth, depends."[15] In naturalism, Lewis continues,

> acts of reasoning are not interlocked with the total interlocking system of Nature as all its other items are interlocked with one another. They are connected with it in a different way; as the understanding of a machine is certainly connected with the machine but not in the way the parts of the machine are connected with each other. The knowledge of a thing is not one of the thing's parts. In this sense something beyond Nature operates whenever we reason.[16]

In this last paragraph, the thrust of Lewis's argument against naturalism becomes clear. By definition, naturalism excludes the possible existence of anything beyond nature, outside the box. But the process of reasoning *requires* something that exceeds the bounds of nature. Of course, the same situation applies in the case of *moral* reasoning; the laws that govern morality must also exist outside the box.

One of naturalism's major problems is explaining how mindless forces give rise to minds, knowledge, sound reasoning, and moral principles that really do report how human beings ought to behave. Not surprisingly, every naturalist wants the rest of us to think that *his* worldview, his naturalism, is a product of *his* sound reasoning.

All things considered, it's hard to see why naturalism is not self-referentially absurd. Before any person can justify his or her acceptance of naturalism on rational grounds, it is first necessary for that person to reject a cardinal tenet of the naturalist position. In other words, the only way a person can provide rational grounds for believing in naturalism is first to cease being a naturalist.

So naturalism has major problems with the first test every worldview must pass, the test of reason. It has additional difficulties with the test of experience. I will pass

[15]Ibid., 18.
[16]Ibid., 25.

over the question of whether naturalism can justify the inferences its adherents so readily draw from our experiences of the outer world; their problems with the laws of logic continue in this case as well. I am more interested in how a *consistent* naturalist deals with our common human experience of our inner world. Any worldview that cannot do justice to what we find in our inner world regarding moral obligation and responsibility, about guilt, about love must also rank low in comparison to the Christian worldview. Some naturalists have recognized the problem they have in this regard and have struggled to come up with some account that does not betray their basic position.

For example, some naturalists have pointed out that a person can be moral without believing in God. While that is true, the more basic question is whether such a person has a foundation for his moral convictions beyond his own preferences or will. All of us would prefer to have neighbors who believe in kindness, decency, and honesty. But if my neighbor's moral beliefs and conduct have their ground in nothing but his preferences, dispositions, or acts of will, there is obviously nothing to prevent those inclinations from leading him to behave in a totally different manner tomorrow. As the British philosopher Hastings Rashdall pointed out almost a century ago,

> We say that the Moral Law has a real existence, that there is such a thing as an absolute [i.e., objective] Morality, that there is something absolutely true or false in ethical judgments, whether we or any number of human beings at any given time actually think so or not. . . . We must therefore face the question *where* such an ideal exists, and what manner of existence we are to attribute to it.[17]

Rashdall rejects the contention that an ideal can exist wholly and completely in any single human consciousness or even in the sum total of all human minds. That would

[17]Hastings Rashdall, *The Theory of Good and Evil* (Oxford: Clarendon Press, 1907), 2:211.

work no better for the moral law than it would for the laws of logic or mathematics. "Only," Rashdall continues,

> if we believe in the existence of a Mind for which the true moral ideal is already in some sense real, a Mind which is the source of whatever is true in our own moral judgments, can we rationally think of the moral ideal as no less real than the world itself. Only so can we believe in an absolute standard of right and wrong, which is as independent of this or that man's actual ideas and actual desires as the facts of material nature. The belief in God . . . is the logical presupposition of an "objective" or absolute Morality. A moral idea can exist nowhere and nohow but in a Mind; an absolute moral ideal can exist only in a Mind from which all Reality is derived. Our moral ideal can only claim objective validity in so far as it can rationally be regarded as the revelation of a moral ideal eternally existing in the mind of God.[18]

Just as naturalism cannot do justice to our moral consciousness, it has problems dealing satisfactorily with other features of our inner world. Christians view guilt as the moral and spiritual equivalent of physical pain. Just as bodily pain warns us that something is wrong in our abdomen or joints, so guilt is a clue to the fact that we are out of sync with the moral and spiritual order. It is logically impossible for a naturalist to treat guilt as anything other than an illusion, psychic disorder, or aberration of some kind. And what can a naturalist possibly say about the Greek word for love that appears in the New Testament—*agape*? *Eros* (eroticism; physical love) can be explained on naturalistic grounds. But what about the kind of self-giving love (*agape*) that is one of life's greatest glories? Naturalists cannot do justice to issues like these so long as they continue to think like naturalists.

Our third worldview test is the test of practice. Can naturalists live out their naturalistic assumptions in their

[18]Ibid., 212.

everyday life without doing violence to what we all regard as essential features of humanity? If people really were consistent naturalists and believed that everything in their world, including their thoughts and values, was only a product of determining physical causes, what kind of life would that be?

As some naturalists observe, nothing in principle prevents any naturalist from choosing to live a decent, honorable, virtuous, and loving life. But that is hardly the question. The real question is why any naturalist should think it important to recommend precisely this kind of life. Did nothing make the choices of the Nazis *really* wrong, for example? Do we condemn the people who hatched the Holocaust only because we *feel* what they did was horrible, even subhuman? If it makes a difference how people live their lives—and it does—is anything within the naturalistic worldview able to explain why they should live one way and not another? It certainly appears as though naturalists live under a constant tension. Their *theory* precludes any appeal to the kinds of values that Christians find central to a truly human existence. But their *practice* shows that they do something quite different. Who can blame us when we conclude that when it comes to *living*, naturalists cheat and borrow aspects of the Christian worldview?

CONCLUSION

Naturalism and the Christian faith are natural enemies in the world of ideas. If one of them is true, the other must be false. Some people reject the Christian faith because they make a religious commitment to naturalism and then find any further interest in Christianity logically impossible (notice how logic keeps creeping into the picture). Other people begin by rejecting Christianity for one reason or another and then naturally gravitate to naturalism.

I have argued in this chapter that it is hard to see how

the selection of naturalism as one's worldview can be a wise or rational act. It looks more like an act of blind faith on the part of people who often seem to lack the ability to trace out the logical implications of that belief system.

But even if naturalism is an inadequate worldview, that fact by itself does not establish the Christian worldview. The world holds many other options. In this book, we have time to examine only one of these other alternatives, namely, the so-called New Age movement that has become so popular for people in the West who find both Christianity and naturalism unsuited to their tastes. We look next at New Age thought.☐

Chapter 8

The New Age Movement

It has become difficult to ignore or overlook the New Age movement. If one spends a few moments browsing in almost any secular bookstore, it is hard to miss the prominent displays of New Age literature, which are almost always far more extensive than the meager selection of works marketed under the almost meaningless label of Christian books. Shoppers in Christian bookstores encounter critical evaluations of the New Age movement throughout the store, many of them grouped among the best-selling books of the month. Ruth Tucker summarizes the prominence of New Age thought by saying:

> The most popular and widely publicized new religion in recent years has been the New Age movement, a difficult-to-define variety of mystical, spiritualistic, and occultic groups that above all else are not *new*. From channeling to crystals to harmonic convergence, celebrities and ordinary citizens have been captivated by this increasingly popular religious trend.[1]

Tucker's aside that the New Age isn't new is a point worth remembering. Almost every facet of the movement is

[1]Ruth Tucker, *Another Gospel* (Grand Rapids: Zondervan, 1989), 319.

a revival of a feature of ancient paganism or an element borrowed from modern religious aberrations such as Theosophy, Swedenborgianism, Transcendentalism, Spiritualism, Christian Science, and New Thought mixed in varied combinations with other elements of Eastern religions. In the hands of some New Age teachers, there is just enough use of Christian language and ideas to confuse poorly grounded Christians.

Many leading apologists of New Age are fully conscious of the worldview dimensions of their religion. This is apparent, for example, in the frequent references to "the Age of Aquarius" language, which reflects the belief that New Age thinking is a new way of looking at things (a worldview) specifically designed to replace outmoded worldviews like the Christian faith.

It is difficult for anyone trained in worldview thinking to get a clear grasp of the major elements of the New Age perspective. The experience is not unlike that of attempting to pick up a handful of sand on a seaside beach. The harder one squeezes the sand, the more it slips through one's fingers. Eventually, one is left holding nothing. Clarity and consistency of thought are two qualities that do not characterize New Age advocates.

A POSSIBLE STARTING POINT

Where is the best place to begin one's investigation of New Age thought? J. Gordon Melton, author of *New Age Encyclopedia*, offers as his starting point the highly personal, subjective, and typically mystical New Age experience that seems to transform New Age followers into different people. As Melton explains,

> New Agers have either experienced or are diligently seeking a profound personal transformation from an old, unacceptable life to a new, exciting future. One prominent model for that transformation is healing, which has given rise to what is possibly the largest

identifiable segment of the movement, the holistic health movement.[2]

Once New Agers have undergone such a transforming experience, many assume that a similar experience can not only transform other individuals but also their society and its culture. Perhaps some even dream that a similar transforming experience could bring about a change of the entire race.

The New Age "experience" and the transformation that accompanies it is more than psychological and social in character. It is, New Agers insist, primarily *religious* in nature. The word *spiritual* is an acceptable synonym. Regardless of what words are used, "the movement is centered upon the experience of a personal spiritual-psychological transformation that is identical to what is generally termed a 'religious experience.' "[3] An experience of this type is the one common element that all New Agers share. Christians will see immediately that the desired transforming experience of New Agers is an obvious counterfeit of the New Birth, a fact that explains why New Agers can be so resistant to Christian evangelism. Why should they need the New Birth when their very different worldview has already given them their own transforming experience?

The New Age experience is said to include deliverance from negative aspects of life, including "dysfunctional exploitative relationships, poverty, illness, boredom, purposelessness, and/or hopelessness."[4] Another negative influence from which New Agers are delivered is what Melton calls the kinds of "oppressive 'orthodox' modes of thought"[5] that occupy such a prominent place in Christianity. In place of such negatives, the New Age disciple finds "new openness and new equalitarian relationships with a sense of abundance, regained vitality and health, excite-

[2]J. Gordon Melton, *New Age Encyclopedia* (Detroit: Gale Research, 1990), xiii.
[3]Ibid.
[4]Ibid.
[5]Ibid.

ment, intensity, new meaning, and new future."[6] To the unwary and unthinking, all this can be very attractive.

The parallel to Christian religious experience is made even stronger when one learns that the transforming experience New Agers seek assumes the form of a profound mystical experience. Such an experience often involves an arduous and lengthy spiritual search that results in a personal crisis of sorts. However, it is important to add that the dramatic mystical experience is not universal among New Age followers. Often, they report, their transformation occurs much more slowly and less dramatically as they simply follow recommended New Age procedures such as meditation, the use of crystals, the search for physical and/or psychic healing, or simply their participation in a seminar on New Age thought.

The transformational experience is not the end but the beginning of a long series of additional experiences and quests that are manifested in a variety of different ways.

THE ROLE OF BELIEFS
IN NEW AGE THOUGHT

Our hope that some set of identifiable New Age beliefs can be found is strengthened by Melton's claim that "the movement does possess an identifiable ideological framework, and [that] members do share a common set of beliefs."[7] But in an obvious slap at Christianity, Melton notes that New Agers reject what they regard as "oppressive orthodox creeds and demands for conformity of belief."[8] While Christianity stresses the importance of the acceptance of a specific set of beliefs, resists changes in its basic beliefs, and suspects people who advocate such changes, "New Age beliefs remain extremely malleable and their elaboration constantly in flux."[9] In other words, there may

[6]Ibid.
[7]Ibid., xv.
[8]Ibid.
[9]Ibid.

be no such thing as a false or unacceptable belief for New Agers. And what may be an important belief for this person at this moment may be replaced, presumably even by a contradictory belief.

Melton adds that whatever *beliefs* may be important at the moment, those beliefs are always less important than the New Ager's *experiences*. The test of New Age beliefs is purely pragmatic, that is, the extent to which "they are functional and helpful."[10] The one constant in New Age beliefs is their tentativeness. This kind of thinking, not surprisingly, holds implications for the New Age view of truth. New Agers believe that Truth (the capital *T* is important here) lies somehow beyond the limits of human knowledge and language; it is never something that can be expressed in human language.

"There are," New Agers believe, "numerous means of arriving at Truth, distinguished by their efficiency more than their rightness."[11] Melton is indifferent to the problem he has created here, however. Since, as he has already admitted, humans can never know what the "Truth" (with a capital *T*) is, how can they possibly know when any practice or belief has brought them closer to the Truth? Does one not have to know the Truth before he can know that he has arrived? But putting this serious problem aside for a while, Melton continues: "Thus, accepting any particular means to Truth, for example, a religion like Christianity, is more a matter of choosing a preferred method from among many equally suitable options than discovering the single best and correct means."[12] Several words summarize Melton's teaching at this point, *relativism* and *pluralism* being two of them. I'll return to the kinds of claims made in this paragraph.

To summarize, New Agers do have a belief system. But, they hasten to add, they are not obliged to insist that their beliefs are *true*. Indeed, they avow, any reli-

[10]Ibid.
[11]Ibid., xv.
[12]Ibid.

gious/spiritual belief is at best only one of many possible ways of arriving at *the* Truth (with a capital *T*). But, given that *the* Truth is unknowable, it is hard to see how anyone could ever come to knowledge that he has arrived at *the* Truth or even, presumably, is on the right path. But since one path is as good as another, this should eventually be no problem, except for the seemingly contradictory claim that some paths are better than others and, what is even worse, that some paths may be downright dangerous.[13]

AN ASSORTMENT OF NEW AGE BELIEFS

Even though the points raised in the previous paragraphs would appear to suggest that every New Age belief is optional, untrue in the traditional sense of *true*, and valued only in its functional ability to bring the New Ager to certain experiences, a quick glance at any list of New Age beliefs suggests a common core that includes many non-optional beliefs. After all, if any New Ager were to abandon many or most of the beliefs we'll be noticing, he would no longer be a New Ager.

Reincarnation and Karma

As we have seen, the New Age goal is a way of life that leads to personal transformation, not simply in some initiatory experience, not simply throughout an entire lifetime, but over the whole course of a spirit's existence, which encompasses many incarnations. Since no path of growth and spiritual development "can be completed in one lifetime," Melton explains, "a common belief in reincarnation and karma provides a long-term framework in which to view individual spiritual progression. Individuals will ac-

[13]According to New Age advocate, George Trevelyan, "All ways lead to the summit, but not all ways suit everyone. Each must choose a way or be thrown into some confusion. And certain of the more direct routes are admittedly dangerous." George Trevelyan, *A Vision of the Aquarian Age* (Walpole, N. H.: Stillpoint Publishing, 1984), 23.

complish their moral and spiritual development as they live out the consequences of prior actions, from this life and previous ones, over a period of successive lifetimes in a physical body."[14]

It would be difficult to find any New Age belief held with more passion and tenacity than this one. Melton observes that some of this passionate attachment to the doctrine results from the intensity with which New Age converts have repudiated Christian beliefs about the afterlife. Moreover, once one abandons a worldview in which one's existence involves a relationship with a personal God, theories of reincarnation and karma offer "explanations" for many of life's negativities and inequalities. We are where we are *now* because of things that happened to us in the earlier, impersonal wheel of existence.

The cyclical view of history and existence that underlies belief in reincarnation and karma was a staple of ancient thinkers like Plato, Aristotle, and the Stoics.[15] The cyclical view of history, reincarnation, and karma have been essential elements of several Eastern religions. The New Testament is clearly opposed to all such thinking. As the epistle to the Hebrews makes clear, Christianity supplants the pagan cyclical view of history with a linear view.[16] History does not repeat itself; history has a beginning and an end. Christ died *once* for the sins of the world. Human beings live but once. It is appointed unto men *once* to die, and after this comes the judgment (Heb. 9:27).

[14]Melton, *New Age Encyclopedia*, xvi.

[15]A point of clarification: I am not suggesting of course that reincarnation and karma were doctrines taught by all these thinkers. The emphasis in my sentence is on the Greek attachment to the cyclical view of history.

[16]See my *The Gospel and the Greeks*, chap. 6.

Universal Energy or Power

New Age posits "a basic energy" that is referred to by many different names[17] and is believed to cause psychic and physical healing. As Melton explains the New Age view, "Members of the New Age Movement assume the existence of a basic energy that is different from the more recognized forms of energy (heat, light, electromagnetism, gravity, etc.) which supports and permeates all of existence."[18] Meditation and physical therapies are thought to release this energy. It is this force that passes between two people who are in love.

Higher Consciousness

New Agers seek a mystical awareness that they sometimes call Christ consciousness. It is important to remember that the "Christ" New Agers refer to is *not* the Christ of the New Testament. Christ for them is not the divine-human person we encounter in the Gospels but a Cosmic Principle. The historical Jesus, New Agers believe, is simply one of many teachers like Gautama Buddha whose teachings will help bring about the New Age.

God

Many, not all, New Agers are pantheists. This means that they believe that everything is one and that this ultimate One is God.[19]

> Once we begin to see that we are all God, that we all have the attributes of God, then I think the whole purpose of human life is to reown the Godlikeness

[17]The names include the following: healing force, orgone energy, odic force, mana, prana, and even holy spirit.

[18]Melton, xvi.

[19]Compare: "The one distinguishing feature in the [coming] World Order will be the credo: 'All is One.'" Jonathan Stone, *SPC Journal* (July 1977).

within us; the perfect love, the perfect wisdom, the perfect understanding, the perfect intelligence, and when we do that, we create back to that old, that essential oneness, which is consciousness.[20]

All human beings, on this view, are really gods. Not surprisingly, though, most humans are ignorant of their identification with God, of the fact that they have lived before this life, and that they will live after this life.

Because everything is interrelated within the being of the same single substance, it follows that "ultimately there is no difference between God, a person, a carrot or a rock. They are all part of one continuous reality that has no boundaries, no ultimate divisions. Any perceived differences between separate entities—between Joe and Judy or between Joe and a tree or between God and Judy—are only apparent and not real."[21]

Biblical Christians disagree. Everything is not one. There is a crucial distinction between the almighty, sovereign Creator and the contingent, finite world that owes its existence to his act of creation. Christians also object to pantheism. Everything is not God.

It is important to note that some strains of New Age thought reject monism and pantheism in favor of a kind of dualism dating back to ancient Gnosticism. This second view of things makes a distinction between the spirit world that is good and the physical world that is evil.[22]

THE NEW AGE WORLDVIEW

Rather than continue this detailed examination of New Age beliefs, it will save time and facilitate understand-

[20]Cited in Francis Adeney, "Educators Look East," *Spiritual Counterfeits Journal* (Winter 1981): 28. The quote comes from New Age teacher Beverly Galyean.
[21]Douglas Groothuis, *Unmasking the New Age* (Downers Grove, Ill.: InterVarsity, 1986), 18.
[22]For an introduction to Gnostic ways of thinking, see my *The Gospel and the Greeks*, Part Three.

ing if major New Age beliefs are simply presented in outline form as part of a chart that contrasts those beliefs with the worldviews of Christianity and naturalism.[23]

	Naturalism	New Age	Christianity
GOD	God does not exist; belief in God results from superstition	Pantheism:[24] God is impersonal, is above good and evil; everything is God	God is the triune, eternal, personal, almighty, sovereign, all-knowing, loving, just and holy Creator
METAPHYSICS	The natural order is eternal, self-sufficient and uncreated. It is ultimately matter/energy	The world is divine	The world was created by God
EPISTEMOLOGY	Human sense experience; the scientific method	Truth lies within every human; it is attained through states of mystical consciousness	Truth has objective standing; it is independent of human desire; functional view of truth is false. Humans can know because God created them as rational creatures
ETHICS	Ethics is relative	Ethics is relative	Ethics is not relative. The moral law grounded in the being of God
HUMANS	Humans are highly evolved animals	Humans are spiritual beings who are gods	Humans are creatures made in the image of God
BASIC HUMAN PROBLEM	Superstition and ignorance	Ignorance of our true human potential	Sinners in rebellion against God
THE SOLUTION TO THE HUMAN PROBLEM	Scientific advancement and technology	Transformation of consciousness	Salvation by faith in the finished work of Christ

[23]The chart is adapted from one that appears in Douglas Groothuis's *Unmasking the New Age*, 167. I have made a number of changes.

[24]For the record, we have already mentioned the minority of New Age followers who seem to follow a type of Gnostic dualism.

			that transforms human nature
DEATH	The end of human existence	An illusion; the entrance to the next life (reincarnation)	The end of our earthly life; heaven for the believer and eternal judgment for the unbeliever
JESUS CHRIST	A merely human teacher	One of many gurus or master teachers who have appeared throughout history	The unique incarnation of God; the only Lord and Savior

While many features of New Age thought are not captured here,[25] this chart gives a broad idea of the New Age worldview. It is clear that New Age thinking conflicts with essential Christian beliefs on every point. And it also contradicts naturalism. Our next task is to see how well this worldview measures up to the tests by which any worldview should be evaluated.

NEW AGE AND THE TEST OF REASON

The New Age movement is in trouble right from the start. A New Age prophet or teacher who is also an advocate of the law of noncontradiction would be a rare bird indeed. Being a New Ager is synonymous with believing that the most important kinds of human consciousness transcend the laws of logic. Not only do New Agers insist on special treatment for the mystical states of consciousness that play such a central role in their movement, their disregard for the laws of logic is also apparent in the relativism they defend in the areas of human knowledge (epistemology) and conduct (ethics).

[25]One of these other features is the frequent practice of channeling, which is supposedly an event in which the spirit of a dead person speaks through a living person (the channeler). America's best known channeler is the Boopsie character in the "Doonesbury" strip. It should be noted that the spirit is seldom that of any person known to us through history.

I refer the reader to my discussion and defense of the law of noncontradiction in chapter four. The law of noncontradiction is simply not an option; it is not something we can take or leave. The principle of noncontradiction is an unavoidable law of thought and being. Either the New Age advocate utilizes the law when he speaks and writes or he does not. If he does not, his claims must be unintelligible. For example, when he says that everything is One, the word *one* must have a definite meaning that excludes its complement. Certainly New Age teachers act as though they and everyone else can know what they mean. If, on the other hand, the New Ager does utilize the law of noncontradiction when he speaks or writes, his disrespect for the law whenever it suits his purposes reveals the arbitrary nature of his claims.

David Clark and Norman Geisler focus on this serious weakness in New Age thinking. *"The critical issue in dealing with New Age thinking,"* they write, *"is its strong aversion to rationality."*[26] They continue by pointing out:

> New Agers resist the conceptual, evidential, and analytic approach to religion and faith. But those who speak with New Agers recognize that every meaningful interaction between two thinking persons requires a common playing field on which the discussion can take place. . . . The ground rules of the game must include rational principles that delimit what both participants will accept as truth and whose ideas have evidence and are "reasonable."[27]

New Agers have many other problems with the laws of logic. Consider, for example, the distressing inconsistency they reveal in their handling of the word *God*. Earlier we noted one New Age teacher making reference to the attributes of God. In other words, New Agers think they know enough about what they call "God" to distinguish

[26]David K. Clark and Norman L. Geisler, *Apologetics in the New Age* (Grand Rapids: Baker, 1990), 223.
[27]Ibid., 223–24.

their god from false or misleading theories about God, their favorite example being Christianity. Before one can know what God is not, he must first know what God is. But the New Age God, we must remember, transcends all the usual human categories. Their god is beyond good and evil, for example. The problems for such a view are serious. Clark and Geisler explain:

> . . . if *God* is a word of which no concepts can be predicated, then *God* has no meaning. We say nothing about God. Our idea of God becomes shapeless and formless. . . . If *God* is without any cognitive shape at all, it is not meaningful to call God good or personal or anything else. Yet some pantheists will in the next breath talk about God in various ways. It is inconsistent to deny concepts of God at one time and at another time to talk about God as if we had some meaningful idea of what *God* means. . . . It is unfair for pantheists to deny any meaningful concept of *God* and then to use the word by plundering meaning from the theist's idea of God.[28]

What the writers are referring to is the fact that New Agers want it both ways: if God is above human knowledge and ideas, then we are unable meaningfully and consistently to apply any predicates to God at all. New Agers insist that God is above human knowledge, yet they continue to speak of he/she/it as though they know what they're talking about.

Another serious inconsistency is present in the relativistic theory of knowledge that pervades New Age thought. Shirley MacLaine reflects this relativism when she says that "everyone has his own truth, and truth, as an objective reality, doesn't exist."[29] Earlier in this chapter, we noticed the New Age conviction that all spiritual paths lead to the same goal. Even though these different paths may appear contradictory, they really are not. But no New Age disciple

[28]Ibid., 227–28.
[29]Shirley MacLaine, quoted in *The New Age Catalog* (New York: Doubleday, 1988), 40. The quote comes from her *It's All in the Playing*.

really believes that all paths are equal. All of them reject at least one spiritual path, that of biblical Christianity. If, as at least one New Age teacher warns, some paths can be dangerous, does that not imply that some paths are wrong? "In the final analysis," Roger Olson points out, "one must wonder whether *any* path leads to the top or whether the 'top' of the mountain—Truth—floats freely in the clouds to be reached only by mystical illumination or channeled messages."[30] The relativism so dear to New Age hearts suffers from a serious inconsistency. Olson says, "In spite of attractive denials of exclusive truth, most New Agers believe that all other worldviews and belief-systems are fundamentally flawed while theirs is the pure wisdom of Higher Knowledge, above rational embrace or criticism."[31]

No one familiar with the whole of the Christian message can deny the central place Christianity gives to inner religious experience, toward directing the soul to God, and toward inner wholeness. But Christianity achieves all this and more without repudiating reason or logic. While Christianity passes the test of reason, New Age thought does not.

NEW AGE AND THE TEST OF EXPERIENCE

In an effort to shorten what is already a long discussion, I will mention only one way that New Age thought fails this test. The New Age movement cannot possibly do justice to questions rising from our experience of evil and suffering. The tendency of New Agers is to deny the reality of both. In her book *Dancing in the Light*, Shirley MacLaine denies the existence of evil. "Everything in life is the result of either illumination or ignorance. These are the two polarities. Not good and evil."[32] Given the basic assump-

---

[30]Roger E. Olson, "Christianity, Coherence and the New Age Movement," *Christian Scholars Review* 20 (1990–1991): 356.
[31]Ibid.
[32]Shirley MacLaine, *Dancing in the Light* (Toronto: Bantam, 1985), 247.

tions of New Age thought, they are forbidden—on pain of inconsistency—to view evil realistically. If God is all, if God encompasses everything, then God's being (whatever it is) must encompass good and evil, thus obliterating any distinction between them. Historic Christianity does not ignore or play games with our inescapable human encounter with evil and suffering.

NEW AGE AND THE TEST OF PRACTICE

Some may think that New Age can hold its own on the test of practice. After all, we have countless testimonies of New Age converts who tell us how they have been delivered from this or that negative, how they have been "saved" from boredom or stress, how they have been raised to a higher level of consciousness. Where once they were failures, they are now successes.

But something very interesting lurks here. How can one really be sure the changes he can see in his life are changes for the better? Progress and improvement must be assessed by a standard of measurement, by an objective and recognizable goal. No one need deny that many New Age people are different from what they once were. But are they better people?

What I'm leading up to is the question whether the New Age movement has an ethic. They talk about values such as "etherialization" and "planetization," which appears to reflect concern for humans and human values. But that is all it is—a façade. Missing from New Age thinking is any cognizance of the necessary role that objective and universal ethical standards play in proper human conduct. Do I have duties to my brothers and sisters within the world community? What are those duties? Where do they come from? If they are as relative as the "truth" New Agers talk about, why should I fulfill those duties? Should human beings really tell the truth? Should they really keep their promises? What is the ground of these moral obligations?

One of the most important things Christians can do to witness to friends who are involved with New Age is to help them see that everyone has limits to his or her tolerance for other people's karma. Enter into a dialogue with your New Age friends about what they would think and do if some other individual (who in their view is as much god as they) should choose to break into their home, steal their property, threaten their children with sexual abuse. Is there no point at which they would scream *"Stop"*?

My point is that the mindless relativism New Agers adopt must, sooner or later, collide with basic human values. When a rapist is about to assault someone you love, you do not sit passively by and wish that he had somehow achieved a state of higher consciousness. Good and evil are not the same, and eventually every human being will find himself in situations that leave him unable to live as though they are. Once we recognize that good and evil are not the same and that truth and error are not the same, we are on our way to reintroducing reason into our lives.

CONCLUSION

How does the New Age movement fare in the battle of worldviews? People outside the New Age circle can answer that more easily than those within. Since naturalists do not consciously repudiate reason, it is at least possible in principle to reason with them. But once someone thinks he has crossed the line into a higher stage of consciousness, words from anyone on the other side of that line are automatically dismissed as the mumblings of the unenlightened.

What could lead educated and sensible people to ignore the pagan roots of New Age practice? Is it possible that New Agers are blind to the dependence of the movement upon earlier systems such as Theosophy and Spiritualism? Can they not see how impossible it is to act and think like human beings without utilizing principles of reason and morality, which they inconsistently repudiate? Fortunately, in *this* battle in the world of ideas, Christians have more than their own private experiences to counter the occultic experiences of the New Ager. Christians also have reason on their side. Christians can live what they believe because, unlike New Agers, Christians do not have to sacrifice logic on the altar of religious transformation or any of the essential guiding principles of life on the altar of moral and epistemological relativism.□

Chapter 9

The Incarnation and the Resurrection

Up to this point, much of what I've said has been to show that assorted attacks upon the reasonableness of Christian faith fail to persuade. I trust it is also clear how the kind of worldview approach developed here tends to build a solid, positive case to support our faith. Sooner or later, however, believers must be prepared to make a case on behalf of two central Christian doctrines, namely, the Incarnation (including the claim that Jesus Christ is both God and man) and the Resurrection of Jesus Christ. Should either be shown to be false, the Christian worldview would suffer a mortal blow. We need to understand how strong the case for these beliefs is.

THE INCARNATION

Christians use the word *incarnation* to express their belief that the birth of Jesus Christ marked the entrance of the eternal and divine Son of God into the human race. Jesus was not simply a human being. Nor is it correct to say that Jesus was merely *like* God. The historic Christian position is that Jesus Christ is fully God and fully man.[1]

[1] The reader will remember our defense in chapter six of this belief against the charge that it involves a logical contradiction.

147

The doctrine of the Incarnation is one of those beliefs that makes Christianity unique among the religions of the world. Christians believe that the sovereign triune God, who can be known only as he chooses to reveal himself, has "made himself known to us, in the most direct and comprehensible way possible, by coming amongst us as one of us, and sharing our life, its heights and depths, its joys and sorrows."[2] He has done this because of his love for humankind.

One recommended way to approach this doctrine suggests that we identify and carefully analyze all reasonable (at least initially reasonable) alternatives to the traditional Christian understanding of Jesus. That way we can evaluate the relative plausibility of each alternative when compared with the belief that Jesus is God incarnate. In other words, suppose I set up a contrast (disjunction) between the belief that Jesus was merely and only a human being (call this belief A) and the historic Christian belief that Jesus is the God-man (belief B). If A presents serious difficulties relative to B, then A should be abandoned in favor of B. Naturally, this does not mean that B (the Christian position) is home free; other challenges await, which we can call C, D, and so on. We must consider each of these in turn. We will discover that belief in the Incarnation (B) not only avoids difficulties faced by the other theories but does a far better job of accounting for assured facts than they do. But let us drop all this abstract theorizing and consider some concrete examples.

The major alternative to the Christian belief in the Incarnation is the claim that Jesus Christ was simply a human being. Of course, as it turns out, even the strongest opponents of the Christian hypothesis are forced to admit that it hardly does justice to Jesus to say that he was just another human being. Most opponents of the Incarnation are willing to acknowledge that Jesus was a remarkable

<hr />

[2]Brian Hebblethwaite, "Jesus, God Incarnate," in *The Truth of God Incarnate*, ed. Michael Green (Grand Rapids: Eerdmans, 1977), 102.

human being, up there with Moses, Gautama, St. Francis of Assisi, Gandhi, and perhaps Mother Teresa. In other words, Jesus was—it seems fair to say—a *good* man. Some adherents of this view might even be willing to say that of all the human beings who have lived, Jesus was possibly the finest, noblest, and most virtuous; they would always add the qualification that this is *all* that he was. He was still only human.

We have, then, what philosophers call a disjunction between *A* and *B*. Either Jesus was merely a good human being (*A*) or Jesus was God incarnate (*B*). Following many others, I am going to argue that *A* makes absolutely no sense. Therefore, according to an elementary and well-known rule of deductive logic, the falsity of *A* establishes the truth of *B*. While we will have to consider the remaining alternatives to the Christian position, we'll discover that none of them holds any more promise.

The falsity of *A*, which we could call the Unitarian thesis, becomes evident when we become familiar with the kinds of things Jesus said and did. A great many of his statements and actions are totally inconsistent with the hypothesis that he was simply a good human being. In assessing these claims and deeds of Jesus, we must remember that he worked within the context of a strict Jewish monotheism, a context in which people who understood his meaning sought to kill him for blasphemy. John Stott provides an account of the many times when Jesus claimed to be God. According to these claims, Stott explains, Jesus taught that

> to know him was to know God;
>
> to see him was to see God;
>
> to believe in him was to believe in God;
>
> to receive him was to receive God;
>
> to hate him was to hate God;
>
> to honor him was to honor God.[3]

[3]John Stott, *Basic Christianity* (Grand Rapids: Eerdmans, 1957), 27. Stott supports his statements with the following verses in the New

One who is merely a good human being does not say things like this. Imagine that you're the parent of two or three children who have become fascinated with the new neighbor down the street. He is clearly a special human being. You and your spouse admire his character. His love for other human beings is manifested in everything he does. You often say that nothing would please you more than that your children should grow up to be just like him.

But then suppose your children come home one day after spending an hour or two with the neighbor and tell you that he said he existed before Abraham,[4] he and God are equal,[5] and at the end of the world he will come on the clouds of the sky, with power and great glory, to judge the nations for their sins.[6] Would you still want your children to grow up to be just like him? Jesus' very words cause us to question whether we should continue to think of him as good.

Jesus' *actions* were also inconsistent with the theory that he was simply a good man. For example, he allowed people to worship him with a reverence that is appropriate only to God.[7] But in an especially subtle kind of example—subtle in the sense that its significance often escapes people until it's pointed out to them—Jesus claimed to have authority to forgive sins. When Jesus forgave people, he went beyond what any of us are able to do. Any of us can forgive people for things they do to *us*. Jesus did that, of course; but he also forgave people for sins they had committed against other people! In all these cases, Jesus acted as though the sins against other human beings were violations of *his* law and sins against him as well.

Testament: Mark 9:37; John 5:23; 8:19; 12:44–45; 14:1, 7, 9; 15:23. This list could be expanded by including Matt. 11:27; John 5:17; 10:30; 14:10–11; 19:7; and many more.

[4]John 8:58.

[5]John 10:30. Jews who heard Jesus say this sought immediately to kill him for blasphemy.

[6]Matt. 24:30 and other verses.

[7]Matt. 16:16 and, for those willing to consider a verse describing a post-resurrection event, John 20:28.

Consider these words from C. S. Lewis:

> Now unless the speaker is God, [the claim to forgive
> sins] is really so preposterous as to be comic. We can
> all understand how a man forgives offenses against
> himself. You tread on my toe and I forgive you, you
> steal my money and I forgive you. But what should we
> make of a man, himself unrobbed and untrodden on,
> who announced that he forgave you for treading on
> other men's toes and stealing other men's money?
> Asinine fatuity is the kindest description we should
> give of his conduct. Yet this is what Jesus did. He told
> people that their sins were forgiven, and never waited
> to consult all the other people whom their sins had
> undoubtedly injured. He unhesitatingly behaved as if
> He was the party chiefly concerned, the person chiefly
> offended in all offenses. This makes sense only if He
> really was the God whose laws are broken and whose
> love is wounded in every sin. In the mouth of any
> speaker who is not God, these words would imply
> what I can only regard as a silliness and conceit
> unrivalled by any other character in history.[8]

The view that Jesus was nothing more than a good
man is in deep trouble! At this point, adherents of the view
begin to make strained moves to ease their difficulties.
Some attempt to argue that Jesus, the good man, never
made the claims that are the source of such embarrassment
to Unitarians. But I'm afraid that won't fly. We know that
the Gospels were written within the lifetime of people who
were eyewitnesses to the things Jesus said and did. In some
instances, like his forgiving sins, the very subtlety of the
point gives it the ring of authenticity. As John Stott
explains, "It is not possible to eliminate these claims from
the teaching of the carpenter of Nazareth. It cannot be said
that they were invented by the evangelists, nor even that
they were unconsciously exaggerated. They were widely
and evenly distributed in the different Gospels and sources

[8]Lewis, *Mere Christianity*, 55.

of the Gospels, and the portrait is too consistent and too balanced to have been imagined."[9]

But what about some of the other alternatives (the options I earlier designated as *C, D,* and so on)? If it doesn't make sense to say that Jesus was just a good man, surely there are other options open to us. Unfortunately for their adherents, the other alternatives appear to face even more objections. One might say that if Jesus wasn't a good man, then perhaps he was an evil man. After all, who but an evil man would attempt to mislead people into worshiping him as God? But of course there is no way to square such an understanding of Jesus with the information we have about him. Perhaps then, others might say, he was insane, a move that allows us to take a more benign attitude toward his character while denying his sanity. Or maybe he was Satan incarnate, hardly a move that would commend itself to skeptics who reject the supernatural.

Lewis has disposed of all these alternatives in a paragraph that has become a classic:

> I am trying here to prevent anyone from saying the really foolish thing that people often say about Him: "I'm ready to accept Jesus as a great moral teacher, but I don't accept His claim to be God." That is the one thing we must not say. A man who was merely a man and said the sort of things Jesus said would not be a great moral teacher. He would either be a lunatic—on a level with the man who says he is a poached egg—or else he would be the Devil of Hell. You must make your choice. Either this man was, and is, the Son of God; or else a madman or something worse. You can shut Him up for a fool, you can spit at Him and kill Him as a demon; or you can fall at His feet and call Him Lord and God. But let us not come with any patronizing nonsense about His being a great human teacher. He has not left that open to us. He did not intend to.[10]

[9]Stott, *Basic Christianity,* 33.
[10]Lewis, *Mere Christianity,* 55–56. Lewis's argument has been caricatured by many who oppose his conclusion; as we know, it's always

Whenever I have presented Lewis's argument to audiences of college students, I have always had one or two in the group offer still another alternative. Perhaps, they suggest, Jesus was simply mistaken. Such people agree that the Jesus of the Bible could not have been merely a good man; and they see quite clearly the unacceptability of theories that treat him as evil or insane. But, their argument goes, surely there are degrees of error this side of lunacy that permit us to retain some respect for Jesus without buying into the Christian view.

The obvious reply that must be made to such a suggestion goes like this: There are little mistakes and then there are big— *really big*—mistakes. Beliefs like "Ron Nash is Cleveland's greatest philosopher" might represent the class of little mistakes; after all, there really is not much competition for this title. Beliefs like "Ron Nash is America's greatest philosopher" would clearly represent a big mistake. But a claim like "Ron Nash (or pick the name of any human being) believes he is God" is a *really* big mistake. Surely those people who intend to pass off Jesus' assertion that he was God as an error so insignificant as to leave our admiration of him untouched make it difficult for others to admire their reasoning powers—at least on this issue.

It is hardly surprising, then, that so many who have looked at this argument concluded that the most sensible choice to make, given the alternatives, is to believe that Jesus Christ is God. Such a decision is not a blind leap of irrational faith—an act made possible only by a suspension of their critical faculties. It is a decision that makes perfectly good and rational sense to anyone whose own

easier to attack straw men. Lewis's argument is not reducible to the "God or lunatic" disjunction claimed by his critics. Lewis argued essentially what I have argued: bring out your alternatives to the Christian hypothesis and we'll consider them one by one. That Jesus was merely a good man is one hypothesis; that he was mad is another. None of the alternatives makes so much sense as the shocking alternative, namely, that Jesus Christ really was God incarnate.

critical faculties are not under the control of naturalistic presuppositions.

If and when a person sees that Jesus Christ is God, important implications follow. For one thing, if Jesus Christ is God, it follows that God exists. In other words, it is possible that the line of reasoning we've been considering in this section may function for some people as an argument for God's existence. Second, if Jesus Christ is God, his teachings are not guesses or mere human speculation; Jesus' words are the Word of God. This means that there really is special revelation in which God reveals truth to human beings.[11] Moreover, if Jesus Christ is God, we have more than a revelation from God in human language. God has revealed *himself*—his person, his nature, his character—in a living way.[12] To know Jesus' teaching is to know God's teaching; to know Jesus' character is to know God's character; to believe in Jesus is to believe in God; to know Jesus is to know God.

Furthermore, consider all the other things we can settle once we know that Jesus is God and that his words are God's words. We then have an authoritative answer to all of our most important questions: Is there a personal God who loves us? What is our duty in life? How do we become children of God? Why did Jesus die? Is there life after death?

Our decision regarding the Incarnation and the deity of Christ turns out therefore to take place at the most important fork in our personal and intellectual quest for truth. As I have shown, a decision *for* the Christian hypothesis is one in which we have reason on our side.[13]

[11]Obviously, this sentence is not claiming that the teachings of Jesus are the only examples of special revelation we have. But they certainly constitute a start. Of course, Jesus taught his disciples to regard the Old Testament as the revealed Word of God. And he also promised that God would reveal the truth that would become what we today know as the New Testament. See John 16:13.

[12]See John 1:1–14 and Hebrews 1:1–2.

[13]Because of its importance, the subject of the Incarnation touches on many other topics that deserve careful study. I recommend *The Truth of God Incarnate*, ed. Michael Green, as a competent, nontechnical place to begin. In my book, *The Gospel and the Greeks*, I discuss and criticize

THE RESURRECTION

The New Testament presents the resurrection of Jesus Christ as a historical event that is supported by the strongest possible eyewitness testimony (1 Cor. 15:5–8). For the apostle Paul, the historicity of the Resurrection is a necessary condition for the truth of Christianity and for the validity of Christian belief (1 Cor. 15:12–19). Paul writes, ". . . if Christ has not been raised, your faith is futile; you are still in your sins. Then those also who have fallen asleep in Christ are lost. If only for this life we have hope in Christ, we are to be pitied more than all men" (1 Cor. 15:17–19).

The Resurrection is the central event of the New Testament. The culmination of each Gospel is the Resurrection. The life of Jesus was presented as a preparation for his death and the Resurrection that followed. Peter's sermon on Pentecost, the birthday of the Christian church, emphasized several times that the Jesus who had died on the cross had been raised from the dead by the power of God. Paul repeatedly explained his otherwise unaccountable conversion to Christianity as a result of his encounter with the risen Christ. A. M. Ramsey writes, "The Gospel without the Resurrection was not merely a Gospel without its final chapter; it was not a Gospel at all. . . . Christian theism is Resurrection theism."[14] According to Alan Richardson,

> The pervading truth which can be learnt from every part of the Gospels, and not merely from their concluding sections, is that the central conviction of the communities in which and for which they were written was faith in Jesus as the Risen Lord; without

numerous attempts to explain away the early Christian belief in the Incarnation. In my book, *Christian Faith and Historical Understanding*, I provide a brief introduction to attempts to undermine confidence in the biblical picture of Jesus through the use of various types of biblical criticism. The literature on these and related subjects is endless.

[14]A. M. Ramsey, *The Resurrection of Christ* (London: Bles, 1945), 7–8.

this faith the Gospels would not have been written. Faith in the resurrection is not one aspect of the New Testament teaching, but the essence of it.[15]

In some parts of Christendom, it has become fashionable to attempt to explain away the miracle of Christ's resurrection. In one such view, Jesus simply continued to live in the hearts of his followers. Such a theory, however, is totally out of step with the New Testament evidence and with historic Christianity, which insists that Christ rose from the dead. The tomb was empty; the risen Christ appeared to his disciples on numerous occasions. These appearances were not hallucinations; the body had not been stolen; Jesus had not simply lost consciousness on the cross and later revived in the tomb. He was dead but now he was alive! Without this fact, it is impossible to explain the existence of the church.

So long as we are not controlled by naturalistic presuppositions, we are able to accept the possibility of miracles; indeed, the miracle of the Resurrection is possible. But when our attention turns to the issue of its actuality, we need to look at the evidence and what that evidence says with regard to the plausibility of alternative explanations. In other words, it makes sense to approach the historicity of the Resurrection using the same method utilized in connection with the Incarnation. Each alternative to the Resurrection can be evaluated as part of an either/or proposition with the belief in the Resurrection on one side and the competing theory on the other. As we discover how each successive alternative is unacceptable for one reason or another, we find that belief in the Resurrection makes more sense—does more justice to the evidence—than the belief that Christ did not rise from the dead.

Any theory that we are to take seriously about what

[15]Alan Richardson, *History, Sacred and Profane* (Philadelphia: Westminster, 1964), 198.

happened following the crucifixion of Jesus must be consistent with the following points:[16]

1. Jesus was dead. One frequently encountered alternative to the Christian belief in the Resurrection holds that Jesus only fainted or lost consciousness on the cross. One can only regard this as an example of wishful thinking on the part of skeptics. The Romans would never have allowed a still-living Jesus to be taken off the cross. The so-called swoon theory assumes that the Romans were so incompetent as to permit a living Jesus to be turned over to his friends. In addition to the excruciating effects of crucifixion, which included not only the spike wounds but also the dislocation of joints and finally the inability to draw breath, Jesus suffered the spear wound to his side. While this wound did not kill him, it provided evidence that he was already dead.

John Stott notes other absurdities of the swoon theory. Are we to believe, he asks,

> that after the rigours and pains of trial, mockery, flogging and crucifixion he could survive thirty-six hours in a stone sepulchre with neither warmth nor food nor medical care? That he could then rally sufficiently to perform the superhuman feat of shifting the boulder which secured the mouth of the tomb, and this without disturbing the Roman guard? That then, weak and sickly and hungry, he could appear to the disciples in such a way as to give them the impression that he had vanquished death? That he could go on to claim that he had died and risen, could send them into all the world and promise to be with them unto the end of time? That he could live somewhere in hiding

[16]It would take an entire book to deal with all the related issues, some of which I must relegate to footnotes that direct the reader to more complete discussions. Some opponents of the Resurrection point to apparent inconsistencies in the Gospel accounts as though these alleged discrepancies are sufficient to cast doubt on the essential point that Jesus was alive. Two excellent discussions of this issue are John Wenham, *The Easter Enigma* (Grand Rapids: Zondervan, 1985), and chapter 8 of George Eldon Ladd's *I Believe in the Resurrection of Jesus* (Grand Rapids: Eerdmans, 1975).

for forty days, making occasional surprise appearances, and then finally disappear without any explanation? Such credulity is more incredible than Thomas's unbelief.[17]

Finally, all such theories stumble over the actual cause of death for victims of crucifixion. The crucified suffered horribly, but it was asphyxiation that finally brought on death. The conditions of crucifixion made it virtually impossible to draw breath, unless the victim could somehow straighten his legs in a way that allowed the chest muscles and the diaphragm to function properly. This explains why the Romans decided to break the legs of the three men who had been crucified that day—to induce asphyxiation, killing the victims and making it possible for everyone to go home.

But when the soldiers came to break the legs of Jesus, they found he was already dead. It is important to note here that the necessarily labored breathing of anyone still alive could not have been missed. Moreover, the collapsed state in which any crucified victim would hang while either unconscious or pretending to be dead would make breathing impossible. One thing is indisputable. Jesus was dead.

2. Following the crucifixion, the disciples were in a state of fear, confusion, and bewilderment. Some opponents of the Resurrection have suggested that the disciples stole the body of Jesus and then concocted the story of the Resurrection. This theory requires a group of strong-willed men who hatched a plot even while Jesus' body was being prepared for burial. The truth is that the disciples were too frightened and confused to think about much more than their own survival as they hid from their enemies. Jesus' death plunged them into such deep despair and fear that the last thing they would have had on their minds was the kind of activity this second theory proposes.

3. Jesus was buried in a new tomb that had been cut into solid rock. The tomb was then closed by rolling a large

[17]Stott, *Basic Christianity*, 49.

stone in front of it. Concerned that the disciples might steal the body of Jesus, Pontius Pilate ordered that a guard be posted to keep the tomb undisturbed and secure.[18] In this way, the enemies of Jesus helped to insure the credibility of the Resurrection by guarding the grave so that no one could steal the body. Of course, some skeptics suggest that even though the friends of Jesus could not have stolen the body of Jesus (because of the guards), the body might have been stolen by the enemies of Jesus. But this is the last thing either the Romans or the Jews would have done. They wanted no further trouble in this matter, something that an empty tomb would have caused. Moreover, even if the enemies of Jesus had stolen the body, they would gladly have produced it as soon as the Christians began preaching the Resurrection.

4. Suddenly Jesus was alive, and the tomb was empty. Alternative theories to the resurrection of Jesus cannot explain the empty tomb. For example, many have said that those who claimed to have seen, heard, and touched Jesus were hallucinating. But we still have to account for the fact that the body of Jesus, which was placed in a closed, sealed, and guarded tomb, was gone. Moreover, these alleged fantasies don't fit the pattern. Hallucinations are not contagious. Had only one or two people claimed to "see" Jesus, it might be possible to dismiss their "experiences" as hallucinations. William Lane Craig points out some of the many things wrong with the hallucination theory:

> First, not just one person but many saw Christ appear. Second, they saw Him not individually, but together. Third, they saw Him appear not just once, but several times. Fourth, they not only saw Him but touched Him, conversed with Him, and ate with Him. Fifth and decisively, the religious enthusiasm hypothesis fails to explain the nonproduction of the body. It would have

[18]See Matthew 27:57–66. While Matthew does not report it, it is hard to believe that a company of soldiers ordered to guard such a tomb would have failed to check first to make certain that the body was in the tomb. It is surely what I would have done.

159

been impossible for Jesus' disciples to have believed in their master's resurrection if His corpse still lay in the tomb. But it is equally incredible to suppose that the disciples could have stolen the body and perpetrated a hoax. Furthermore, it would have been impossible for Christianity to come into being in Jerusalem if Jesus' body were still in the grave. The Jewish authorities would certainly have produced it as the shortest and completest answer to the whole affair. But all they could do was claim that the disciples had stolen the body. Thus, the hypothesis of religious enthusiasm [the hallucination theory], in failing to explain the absence of Jesus' corpse, ultimately collapses back into the hypothesis of conspiracy and deceit, which . . . has pretty much been given up in view of the evident sincerity of the apostles, as well as their character and the dangers they underwent in proclaiming the truth of Jesus' resurrection.[19]

Hallucinations typically require a prepared receiver, someone who wants to see something or who expects to see something. The disciples were not psychologically prepared for such a hallucination. The last thing any of them expected to see was a living Jesus.

The eyewitness testimony for the Resurrection is exceptionally strong. For one thing, the people who claimed to see Jesus were individuals of unimpeachable character. Records of this eyewitness testimony come very early in the history of the Christian movement.[20] Accounts of the Resurrection are not a legend that began circulating years later. It is testimony based on eyewitness accounts that can be located in the years immediately following the event and

[19]William Lane Craig, *Apologetics, An Introduction* (Chicago: Moody, 1984), 174.
[20]Even though Paul's conversion, based as it was on his own encounter with the living Christ, came very early in the history of the Christian movement, Paul made it clear that the Resurrection message that was central in his preaching had been received from others (1 Cor. 15:3). As far as raw numbers go, the number of eyewitnesses exceeded five hundred (1 Cor. 15:6).

publicly proclaimed during the lifetime of people who were alive when the events occurred.

5. Eyewitnesses of the Resurrection suddenly were transformed. Immediately following the death of Jesus, the terrified disciples hid behind locked doors, fearful that they would be the next to die. But on Pentecost, just a few weeks later, these same men boldly and publicly preached the Resurrection. No longer afraid to die, most of them were martyred for their faith, especially for their conviction that Christ had risen. One of the major pieces of evidence that alternatives to the Resurrection must explain is the origin of the Christian church. If the Resurrection never happened, what power or experience transformed that small band of terrified disciples into men and women who were willing to suffer torture and horrible deaths because of their refusal to renounce the Resurrection? What changed them into bold men and women whose evangelistic efforts carried the gospel to every corner of the Roman world and beyond?

A considerable body of additional evidence remains— both direct and circumstantial—that I do not have time to discuss.[21] But the thing to which we keep returning is the fact that good, honorable, trustworthy people who had nothing to gain and everything earthly to lose believed that Jesus had risen bodily from the dead. As George Eldon Ladd says, "Here we are on bedrock. It is impossible to question the facticity of the disciple's belief in Jesus' resurrection."[22] But then we must ask, "What is the *historical* cause of this faith? What historical event caused them to believe that

[21]Of course, there are also other alternatives to the Resurrection that I have not had time to mention. For more complete discussions, I commend the reader to such books as the following: George Eldon Ladd, *I Believe in the Resurrection of Jesus*; my *Christian Faith and Historical Understanding*; William Lane Craig, *Apologetics, An Introduction*; Terry Miethe, ed., *Did Jesus Rise From the Dead?* (San Francisco: Harper and Row, 1987); J. N. D. Anderson, *The Evidence for the Resurrection* (Downers Grove, Ill.: InterVarsity, 1966); Gary Habermas, *The Resurrection of Jesus: An Apologetic* (Grand Rapids: Baker, 1980); and scores of other good sources.

[22]Ladd, *I Believe in the Resurrection*, 24.

Jesus has risen from the dead?"[23] What hypothesis best explains the belief of the early church that the Resurrection had really happened? "All the evidence," Alan Richardson argues, "points to the judgment that the Church did not create the belief in the resurrection of Christ; the resurrection of Christ, historically speaking, created the Church by calling faith into being."[24] In other words, only the *actual Resurrection* is sufficient to explain the faith of the early disciples and the subsequent origin of the Christian church.

William Lane Craig sums things up well when he writes:

> Numerous lines of historical evidence prove that the tomb of Jesus was found empty by a group of His women followers. Furthermore, no natural explanation has been offered that can plausibly account for this fact. Second . . . several lines of historical evidence [establish] that on numerous occasions and in different places Jesus appeared physically and bodily alive from the dead to various witnesses. Again, no natural explanation in terms of hallucinations can plausibly account for these appearances. And finally . . . the very origin of the Christian faith depends on belief in the resurrection. Moreover, this belief cannot be accounted for as the result of any natural influences. These three great, independently established facts—the empty tomb, the resurrection appearances, and the origin of the Christian faith—all point to the same unavoidable conclusion: that Jesus rose from the dead.[25]

This is not a claim that modern men and women find easy to accept; it was not, for that matter, a claim that the citizens of Jerusalem found easy to accept when they first heard it from the lips of the disciples. But it is the claim that best explains all we know about what happened following the death of Jesus.

[23]Ibid., 25.
[24]Richardson, *History, Sacred and Profane*, 200.
[25]Craig, *Apologetics*, 205.

CONCLUSION

The worldview known as naturalism denies the possibility of miracles, that is, events within the natural order caused by a supernatural being existing outside of that order (the box) that upset our normal expectations of how things should be. But the naturalist cannot prove the scientific impossibility of miracles, any more than he can prove the truth of naturalism. Hence, or so I have argued, miracles are, at the very least, possible events.

In this chapter, I have gone beyond the simple claim that miracles are possible and examined the evidence for two miracles on which the Christian worldview places great emphasis—the Incarnation and the Resurrection. When one sets aside the presuppositions of the naturalistic worldview, places oneself within a worldview in which the universe is open to the causal influence of the sovereign, personal God, and honestly examines alternatives in the light of the evidence, he or she may well discover that this system (the Christian worldview) demonstrates all that is required for consistency with reason and with what we know about the world.

If these miracles never happened, the Christian worldview is in deep trouble. But *that* case has yet to be made. If these miracles did happen (and we have reviewed the abundant support for their historicity), the case for the Christian worldview has been greatly strengthened.☐

Chapter 10

Winning the Battle in the World of Ideas

Throughout this book, I have defended a worldview, a conceptual system, a way of looking at God, self, and the world. In this defense, I have stressed the importance of evaluating worldviews on the basis of several tests. One of those tests is logic; logical inconsistency is a sure sign of error. Though some of its critics have accused Christian theism of internal inconsistency in one way or another, the charges don't hold up. Naturalism and the New Age movement, on the other hand, appear to have more than they can handle on this score.

Another important test for any worldview is experience. Here, we found, worldviews should fit what we know about the world outside us and the world we find within us. Christian theism passes this test. As philosopher C. Stephen Evans expresses the result of his own investigation, "Belief in God is genuinely coherent with all we know about ourselves and our universe. It contradicts no known facts and it makes sense of many things that would otherwise be inexplicable."[1] The Christian does not have to pretend that there are no objective moral laws or that one

[1] C. Stephen Evans, *Quest for Faith* (Downers Grove, Ill.: InterVarsity Press, 1986), 131.

does not sometimes feel like thanking God or calling on God for help. The Christian does not have to borrow important beliefs from another system. The Christian's belief structure explains why he or she and other humans often feel a sense of duty, a sense of guilt, a longing for eternal life, and a desire for forgiveness.

Christian theism also passes the important practical test. It is a system of beliefs that people can live and live consistently.

In short, Christian theism is a system that commends itself to the whole person. But all this is only part of the story. Christian theism is a system, but it is also more than that. Therefore, it requires more of human beings than mere intellectual assent to a set of propositions. Most people recognize that there is a difference between *belief that* and *belief in*. It is one thing to *believe that* some proposition is true; it is another thing to *believe in* a person.[2]

In this connection, Christian theism announces that it is a system with a Person at its center. As John Stott explains,

> Christianity is Christ. The person and work of Christ are the rock upon which the Christian religion is built. If he is not who he said he was, and if he did not do what he said he had come to do, the foundation is undermined and the whole superstructure will collapse. Take Christ from Christianity, and you disembowel it; there is practically nothing left. Christ is the centre of Christianity; all else is circumference.[3]

C. Stephen Evans points out what must come next:

> There is a gap between an intellectual recognition of who Jesus is and a commitment to him. Logically, it would seem that anyone who admits that Jesus is the Son of God should be willing to follow him and obey

[2]In other writings, I argue that *belief in* requires *belief that*; the subjective act of commitment requires an objective ground of information. See my *Christian Faith and Historical Understanding*, chap. 8.

[3]John Stott, *Basic Christianity*, 21.

him. It is a truth which ought to transform their lives. But in fact there are many people who will give at least verbal assent to the proposition "Jesus is God," but who do not seem to care very much about Jesus, or even pay him much attention. It is clear then that what is necessary to become a Christian is not merely acceptance of a proposition on the basis of evidence, but *a change in a person's whole orientation to life.*[4]

Evans is right. Many people who *believe that* the essential claims of Christian theism are true have never taken the additional step of coming to *believe in* the divine Person whose incarnation, death, and resurrection are the point to the whole thing. In this connection, it is interesting to remember what the apostle Paul wrote in his epistle to the Romans: ". . . if you confess with your mouth, 'Jesus is Lord,' and believe in your heart that God raised him from the dead, you will be saved" (10:9). In these words, Paul ties the solution to the basic human problem—our alienation from God because of sin and its consequences—to the two indispensable miracles discussed in the last chapter. The reference to the Resurrection is impossible to miss. What may be less clear is Paul's meaning when he speaks of *confessing Jesus as Lord*: acknowledging that Jesus is God. When we confess Jesus as Lord and God, we are acknowledging that nothing else, including ourselves, will function as God in our lives. And when we believe *in our hearts* that God raised Jesus from the dead, we cross the line from a purely intellectual assent to a proposition to a commitment of the entire self to the Person who is both risen Savior and Lord.

Up to this point in the chapter, I have been summarizing what must be believed and what must happen for a person to become part of the family of God. All of this is a first step in doing battle on behalf of the risen Christ and his saving gospel in the world of ideas. It would not make much sense for people to become engaged in that battle so

[4]Evans, *Quest for Faith*, 74.

long as they lack assurance that they are truly part of Christ's church.

The next step—after assurance of salvation—in winning the battle in the world of ideas is understanding the agenda and the message that has been the major burden of this book. That includes grasping the importance and nature of worldview thinking, the content of the Christian worldview, the details of the worldviews that challenge us, and the philosophical and theological tools that this book has introduced. The most effective way to wage the battle in the world of ideas is to do it on the level of worldviews.

But even the best-trained people in worldview thinking are not yet prepared to win the battle in the world of ideas. A final set of lessons remains, which we must take to heart. Those lessons are contained in the same Scripture text I quoted at the beginning, Ephesians 6:10–18:

> Finally, be strong in the Lord and in his mighty power. Put on the full armor of God so that you can take your stand against the devil's schemes. For our struggle is not against flesh and blood, but against the rulers, against the authorities, against the powers of this dark world and against the spiritual forces of evil in the heavenly realms. Therefore put on the full armor of God, so that when the day of evil comes, you may be able to stand your ground, and after you have done everything, to stand. Stand firm then, with the belt of truth buckled about your waist, with the breastplate of righteousness in place, and with your feet fitted with the readiness that comes from the gospel of peace. In addition to all this, take up the shield of faith, with which you can extinguish all the flaming arrows of the evil one. Take the helmet of salvation and the sword of the Spirit, which is the word of God. And pray in the Spirit on all occasions with all kinds of prayers and requests.

The apostle has included a great deal in this passage. Consider only the following points: (1) You are part of a conflict that is often not visible to the human eye; (2) God has provided everything you'll need to come through this struggle successfully; (3) but to be successful, you must put on the armor, the protection, that God has provided; (4) be sure to stand firm; don't waver; don't let someone knock you off your feet; (5) remember that the first element of God's armor is truth.

We do not have to be afraid of any truth in any field since God himself is the author of all truth. Do not think that you have to run from science or philosophy or anything else in order to protect your faith. All truth is God's truth.

(6) Never forget the breastplate of righteousness. The battle is not merely an intellectual one. You are not going to do well in this conflict if your character and moral life fall short of God's standards. (7) Confidence in the Gospel gives us ability to act and move. (8) Your faith in Christ is a shield that can protect you from whatever arrows are shot in your direction. (9) The helmet of salvation is an important part of your armor. If you have doubts about your salvation, the enemy will exploit the openings that these doubts give him. (10) Never ignore the sword of the Spirit. Study God's inspired Word. Let the truth of that Word guide and encourage you and give you wisdom. (11) Finally, pray in the Spirit. Keep your lines of communication with God open. Share your fears and needs with him on a regular basis and let him demonstrate his power as he answers your prayers.

CONCLUSION

Most of us know people who rushed to battle in the world of ideas who lacked the proper grounding in intellectual issues or ignored the armor Paul describes in Ephesians 6. Most forays like this end in disaster—either for the cause of the Gospel or in some cases for the overzealous but unprepared Christian soldier.

Most of us also know Christians who seem afraid to venture out in the intellectual war zones of the day. It may be better in such matters to err on the side of caution. But if you are a Christian who suffers from timidity or self-consciousness or fears your lack of preparation for this sort of thing, I would like to think that this book will give you enough of a basic training in worldview thinking that you can at least hold your own in your first, faltering efforts to accomplish something in the world of ideas.

This book is hardly sufficient by itself to give you everything you need. No book could hope to do that. But it does lay a foundation. Once that foundation has become part of you, why not begin to dialogue with your friends and non-friends about their worldview and yours. Why don't you take those first steps toward winning the battle in the world of ideas?☐

Suggestions for Further Reading

Rather than provide a long list of book titles, this short bibliography will identify a small number of books and tell how they might be useful. The books will be grouped under several headings.

BOOKS PROVIDING A GENERAL INTRODUCTION TO WORLDVIEW THINKING

Clark, Gordon H. *A Christian View of Men and Things*. Grand Rapids: Eerdmans, 1952. An early, philosophically competent analysis of the Christian worldview that includes helpful discussions of epistemology, political theory, and the philosophy of history. A bit advanced for many readers.

Geisler, Norman L., and William D. Watkins. *Worlds Apart: A Handbook on Worldviews*. 2d ed. Grand Rapids: Baker, 1989. An introduction to worldview thinking that focuses on competing views of God.

Nash, Ronald H. *Faith and Reason: Searching for a Rational Faith*. Grand Rapids: Zondervan, 1988. Written as a college textbook, *Faith and Reason* explores in greater detail most of the issues covered in the present book. It includes detailed analyses of several arguments for God's existence as well as a defense of miracles.

Phillips, W. Gary, and William E. Brown. *Making Sense of Your World from a Biblical Viewpoint*. Chicago: Moody, 1991. A helpful, easily understood introduction to a number of problems from a worldview perspective.

Sire, James W. *The Universe Next Door*. 2d ed. Downers Grove, Ill.: InterVarsity, 1988. A widely used introduction to worldview thinking that is especially helpful in its discussions about naturalism and New Age thinking.

BOOKS DEALING WITH NATURALISM

Most of the books already noted contain chapters on naturalism.

Bube, Richard. *The Human Quest: A New Look at Science and the Christian Faith*. Waco: Word, 1971. One of the better books to read when dealing with problems where science and Christianity appear to conflict.

Jaki, Stanley. *The Road to Science and the Ways to God*. Chicago: Univ. of Chicago Press, 1978. Jaki is a Roman Catholic priest who is also trained in science. His books are always thought provoking and supportive of historic Christian thinking.

Noebel, David. *Understanding the Times*. Manitou Springs, Colo.: Summit Press, 1991. This is a massive book equally helpful in introducing one to the Christian worldview and in critiquing Marxism and secular humanism.

Ratzsch, Del. *Philosophy of Science*. Downers Grove, Ill.: InterVarsity, 1986. It is difficult to write anything about the philosophy of science that is both competent and intelligible. This book succeeds.

SOME BOOKS DEALING WITH THE NEW AGE MOVEMENT

Chandler, Russell. *Understanding the New Age*. Waco: Word, 1989. A clearly written introduction to a complex subject.

Groothuis, Douglas R. *Confronting the New Age.* Downers Grove, Ill.: InterVarsity, 1988. The second of two books by this author on the subject of New Age thinking, this work provides help in countering the New Age challenge.

————. *Unmasking the New Age.* Downers Grove, Ill.: InterVarsity, 1986. A best-seller that many readers have found helpful.

Tucker, Ruth. *Another Gospel: Alternative Religions and the New Age Movement.* Grand Rapids: Zondervan, 1989. A good introduction to New Age thinking and other cults.

OTHER BOOKS

Bush, L. Russ. *A Handbook for Christian Philosophy.* Grand Rapids: Zondervan, 1991. Just what its title suggests: an introduction to a variety of philosophical topics that will help ground the reader in a number of important areas.

Nash, Ronald. *Christian Faith and Historical Understanding.* Dallas: Probe/Word Books, 1984. Sooner or later worldview debates get around to questions concerning the historical accuracy of the New Testament. This introduction to the philosophy of history also deals with such historical challenges.

————. *The Christian Parent and Student Guide to Choosing a College.* Brentwood, Tenn: Wolgemuth & Hyatt, 1989. One of the more important contexts in which worldview thinking is demanded is the college setting. This book offers concrete advice to parents and students about how to select a college and then how to get prepared for the intellectual challenges that student will encounter in college.

————. *The Gospel and the Greeks.* Dallas: Probe/Word, 1992. Some of the more deceptive challenges to the Christian worldview involve claims that early Christianity was influenced by pagan philosophical and religious movements. This book examines the evidence and answers the arguments.

———. *Poverty and Wealth*. Dallas: Probe/Word, 1992. Probably no aspect of the Christian worldview is less understood than economics. This book examines economics in a sound, professional way and then relates it to the concerns of the Christian worldview.

———. *The Word of God and the Mind of Man*. Phillipsburg, N. J.: Presbyterian and Reformed, 1992. Fooling people into thinking that God cannot reveal truth to human beings is the quickest way to undermine confidence in the Christian worldview. This book is one of only two or three still in print that defend Scripture from such attacks.

Index

Abraham, W. J., 20, 46
Adams, R. M., 42
Alston, W. P., 17
Aristotle, 16, 28, 84, 103, 136
Armor, Christian, 11, 167–68
Augustine, 21, 36, 37–38, 39, 51
Axioms, 22
Ayer, A. J., 84

Barth, K., 76
Battles in world of ideas, 9–13, 166, 167, 169
Bible, 35, 38, 44, 45, 46, 52, 53, 65, 70, 79, 80, 154, 167
Blanshard, B., 85
Boundary, law as the, 78–79
Bultmann, R., 36

Calvin, J. 27, 40
Carnell, E. J., 61, 71
Casuistry, 45
Certainty, 64, 70–72
Channeling, 140
Christianity, nature of, 32–33, 37
Christian Science, 58–59
Christie, A., 67
Church, 47
Clark, D., 141, 142
Clark, G. H., 54, 55, 82, 164
Clifford, W. K., 88–89, 90–91
Concern, ultimate, 27
Conceptual scheme, 16, 18, 53, 55, 164
Craig, W. L., 159–60, 162
Creation ex nihilo, 35–36, 119, 121, 139
Crucifixion, 38

Davis, S., 118–19
Decalogue, 43

Deduction, 64–65
Deism, 36
Dennis, L., 63
Descartes, R., 39
Despair, 49, 50, 51
Determinism, 85–86, 118–19, 128
Dooyweerd, H., 24, 78–80
Doyle, A. C., 67
Dualism, 27, 61, 76, 138, 139

Empiricism, 38–39, 59
Epistemology, 21, 23, 29, 37–40, 76–79, 139
Ethics, 21, 23, 29–30, 40–46, 60–61, 139, 144–45
   situation, 45–46
Evidentialism, 88–92
Evil, 94–99, 106, 107–115, 144
   free will defense, 108–109
   gratuitous, 111–113
   natural law defense, 109–110
   soul-making defense, 110–111
Experience, test of, 57–62

Gaede, S. D., 116
Geisler, N., 141–42
Genetic fallacy, 87, 124
Gnosticism, 12, 138, 139
God, 24, 26–28, 32, 34–35, 36, 39, 40–41, 46–47, 50, 51, 61, 85, 90, 93, 102–3, 105, 127, 136, 139, 147, 167–68
   evil and, 94–99, 1106, 108, 110–11, 113–14
   existence of, 52–53
   knowledge of, 74–79
   logic and, 74–80
   Naturalism and, 118–21

New Age view of, 137–39, 141–42
Greater good defense, 108–115
Groothuis, D., 138, 139

Halverson, W., 52, 118–19
Hebblethwaite, B., 148
Henry, C. F. H., 52, 77
Higher consciousness, 137, 144–45
History, cyclical views of, 136
Human,
  fully, 104–5
  merely, 104–5
Humankind, 30, 46–51, 103, 139

Ideals, 31
Image of God, 39, 40–41, 46–47, 79, 139
Incarnation, 35, 93, 99–105, 106, 147–154
Induction, 64–69
Innate ideas, 39–40
Inner world, 59–62

Jesus Christ, 35, 47, 51, 69, 70, 93, 99–100, 102, 104, 105, 139, 140, 147–63, 165–66
  in New Age thought, 137
  Resurrection of, 71, 155–163
Kalsbeek, L., 78–79
Karma, 135–36, 145
Kierkegaard, S., 48, 50
Knowledge, 29, 37–40

Ladd, G. A., 157, 161
Leibniz, G., 39
Lewis, C. S., 25, 30, 41, 60–61, 117, 122–25, 151–53
Logic, 74–84, 92, 106, 125, 128, 140, 144, 145, 148
Logical Positivism, 84–85
Love, 43, 45–46, 127
Lucas, J. R., 86

Mackie, J. L., 95, 98
MacLaine, S., 142, 143
Maitland, F. W., 66, 67
Marxism, 8–9, 31, 74
Materialism, 61, 86–88, 116, 119
Mavrodes, G., 17
Melton, J. G., 131–34, 136–37

Metaphysics, 21, 23, 28, 35–37, 139
Methodology, 63–69
Miracles, 117, 119, 120, 163
Mitchell, B., 65
Moral law, 41–42, 60–61, 126–27
Moreland, J. P., 86–87
Morris, T., 22, 62–63, 68–69, 100–5
Mysticism, 74–76, 133

Nagel, E., 66
Nash, R., 12, 28, 29, 32, 34, 35, 37, 38, 39, 59, 63, 69, 78, 84, 89, 93, 98, 110, 111, 121, 153, 154, 155, 165
Naturalism, 8, 36, 58, 85, 86, 88, 114, 116–29, 139–40, 156, 163, 164
Necessity, 39, 123
New Age, 74, 114, 129, 130–46, 164
  ethics of, 144, 145
Noncontradiction, law of, 13, 55–57, 74, 80–84, 93–106, 140–43

Olson, R., 143
Outer world, 58–59
Owen, H. P., 86

Pantheism, 34, 61, 74, 114, 139, 142
Pascal, B., 47
Paul, 10–11, 25, 42, 43, 44, 50, 155, 160, 166
Peter, 155
Peterson, M., 109
Physicalism, 86–88
Plantinga, A., 40, 79–80, 85, 90, 94–99, 107–8
Plato, 16, 28, 35–36, 38, 136
Practice, Test of, 62–63, 65
Presuppositions, 21–23, 63
Principles, 42–46
Probability, 65–72
Process theology, 34
Properties,
  essential and nonessential, 102–103

175

essential and common, 103–104

Purtill, R., 111

Quinn, P., 41

Ramsey, A. M., 155
Rashdall, H., 126
Rationalism, 38, 73
Reality, ultimate, 28, 35–37
Reason, 14, 74–84, 92, 123, 125
    test of, 55–57, 73–92, 93–106
Reincarnation, 135–136
Relativism, 139, 140, 142, 145, 146
Resurrection of Christ, 155–63
Revelation, 37, 51–53, 154
Richardson, A., 155, 162
Roberts, R., 51
Rosetta Stone, 17
Rowe, W., 99
Rules, 42–46
Russell, B., 88

Schaeffer, F., 22, 62–63
Self-referential absurdity, 56, 80, 84–92, 125
Sense experience, 37–39, 59, 73
Sin, 40, 47, 48, 50, 139, 150, 151
Skepticism, 40, 54, 55–56, 77, 79, 84
Solipsism, 55–56
Stace, W. T., 74–76
Stone, J., 137
Stott, J., 48, 149, 151, 157, 165

Tennant, F. R., 109
Test of experience, 57–62
Test of practice, 62–63, 165
    and naturalism, 127–28
    and New Age, 144–45
Test of reason, 55–57, 73–106, 164
    and naturalism, 122–25
    and New Age, 140–43
Theism, 34, 42, 54, 119, 165
Theoretical thought and its foundations, 23–26
Tillich, P., 36
Touchstone proposition, 51–53, 54
Torrance, T., 76–78, 80
Trevelyan, G., 135
Truth,
    necessary, 39, 123
    of propositions, 64, 79, 139
    in New Age movement, 134–35, 139, 142–43
Tucker, R., 130

Validity, 64, 79

Westminster Confession, 48
Worldview,
    Christian, 13, 27, 34–53, 74
    tests of, 13–14, 54–63, 164–165
    nature of, 16–33
    importance of, 17–18, 167
    Christianity as, 19–21, 23
    elements of, 26–32
    and evil, 113–15